The Explosion of TWA Flight 800

The Explosion of TWA Flight 800

Belinda Friedrich

CHELSEA HOUSE PUBLISHERS
Philadelphia

Frontispiece: A distraught U.S. Coast Guardsman leans over the retrieved tail of TWA Flight 800. The entire nation mourned the deaths of 230 passengers in the 1996 plane crash.

CHELSEA HOUSE PUBLISHERS

Editor in Chief Sally Cheney
Associate Editor in Chief Kim Shinners
Production Manager Pamela Loos
Art Director Sara Davis
Production Editor Diann Grasse

Staff for THE EXPLOSION OF TWA FLIGHT 800

Senior Editor LeeAnne Gelletly
Assistant Editor Brian Baughan
Cover Designer Keith Trego
Layout by 21st Century Publishing and Communications, Inc.

First Printing

1 3 5 7 9 8 6 4 2

The Chelsea House World Wide Web address is
http://www.chelseahouse.com

Library of Congress Cataloging-in-Publication Data

Friedrich, Belinda
    The explosion of TWA flight 800 / Belinda Friedrich.
      p. cm. — (Great disasters, reforms and ramifications)
    Includes bibliographical references and index.
    Summary: Explores the 1996 explosion of a 747 jet plane off the coast of Long Island, New York, focusing on the investigation which led to new safety recommendations for fuel tank systems.
    ISBN 0-7910-6325-9 (alk. paper)
    1. TWA Flight 800 Crash, 1996—Juvenile literature. 2. Aircraft accidents—New York (State)—Long Island Region—Juvenile literature. 3. Aircraft accidents—North Atlantic Ocean—Juvenile literature [1. Aircraft accidents.] I. Title. II. Series.

TL553.5 .F76 2001
363.12'465'0974721—dc21   2001042450

Contents

GREAT DISASTERS
REFORMS and RAMIFICATIONS

Jill McCaffrey
National Chairman
Armed Forces Emergency Services
American Red Cross

Introduction

Disasters have always been a source of fascination and awe. Tales of a great flood that nearly wipes out all life are among humanity's oldest recorded stories, dating at least from the second millennium B.C., and they appear in cultures from the Middle East to the Arctic Circle to the southernmost tip of South America and the islands of Polynesia. Typically gods are at the center of these ancient disaster tales—which is perhaps not too surprising, given the fact that the tales originated during a time when human beings were at the mercy of natural forces they did not understand.

To a great extent, we still are at the mercy of nature, as anyone who reads the newspapers or watches nightly news broadcasts can attest.

Hurricanes, earthquakes, tornados, wildfires, and floods continue to exact a heavy toll in suffering and death, despite our considerable knowledge of the workings of the physical world. If science has offered only limited protection from the consequences of natural disasters, it has in no way diminished our fascination with them. Perhaps that's because the scale and power of natural disasters force us as individuals to confront our relatively insignificant place in the physical world and remind us of the fragility and transience of our lives. Perhaps it's because we can imagine ourselves in the midst of dire circumstances and wonder how we would respond. Perhaps it's because disasters seem to bring out the best and worst instincts of humanity: altruism and selfishness, courage and cowardice, generosity and greed.

As one of the national chairmen of the American Red Cross, a humanitarian organization that provides relief for victims of disasters, I have had the privilege of seeing some of humanity's best instincts. I have witnessed communities pulling together in the face of trauma; I have seen thousands of people answer the call to help total strangers in their time of need.

Of course, helping victims after a tragedy is not the only way, or even the best way, to deal with disaster. In many cases planning and preparation can minimize damage and loss of life—or even avoid a disaster entirely. For, as history repeatedly shows, many disasters are caused not by nature but by human folly, shortsightedness, and unethical conduct. For example, when a land developer wanted to create a lake for his exclusive resort club in Pennsylvania's Allegheny Mountains in 1880, he ignored expert warnings and cut corners in reconstructing an earthen dam. On May 31, 1889, the dam gave way, unleashing 20 million tons of water on the towns below. The Johnstown Flood, the deadliest in American history, claimed more than 2,200 lives. Greed and negligence would figure prominently in the Triangle Shirtwaist Company fire in 1911. Deplorable conditions in the garment sweatshop, along with a failure to give any thought to the safety of workers, led to the tragic deaths of 146 persons. Technology outstripped wisdom only a year later, when the designers of the luxury liner *Titanic* smugly declared their state-of-the-art ship "unsinkable," seeing no need to provide lifeboat capacity for everyone onboard. On the night of April 14, 1912, more than 1,500 passengers and crew paid for this hubris with their lives after the ship collided with an iceberg and sank. But human catastrophes aren't always the unforeseen consequences of carelessness or folly. In the 1940s the leaders of Nazi Germany purposefully and systematically set out to exterminate all Jews, along with Gypsies, homosexuals, the mentally ill, and other so-called undesirables. More recently terrorists have targeted random members of society, blowing up airplanes and buildings in an effort to advance their political agendas.

The books in the GREAT DISASTERS: REFORMS AND RAMIFICATIONS series examine these and other famous disasters, natural and human made. They explain the causes of the disasters, describe in detail how events unfolded, and paint vivid portraits of the people caught up in dangerous circumstances. But these books are more than just accounts of what happened to whom and why. For they place the disasters in historical perspective, showing how people's attitudes and actions changed and detailing the steps society took in the wake of each calamity. And in the end, the most important lesson we can learn from any disaster—as well as the most fitting tribute to those who suffered and died—is how to avoid a repeat in the future.

Final Destination

T he 16 students and 5 adult chaperones from the Montoursville High School French Club had been anticipating their trip to Paris, France, for some months. The students were especially excited about the trip and couldn't wait to board the plane. It was July 17, 1996, and they were scheduled for the TWA Flight 800 departing from New York City at 7:00 P.M.

Some of the chaperones seemed to have mixed feelings about going away. Phillip Yothers, the bus driver taking the group from Mountoursville, Pennsylvania, to the John F. Kennedy Airport (JFK), had overheard earlier that day a conversation between Deborah and Douglas Dickey, two of the French club's chaperones. They would really have preferred not to be going to Paris. They had to leave their two young children with grandparents to look after them, and were a bit anxious about how the arrangement would work out. But by the time the bus arrived at Kennedy Airport, the enthusiasm of the students was contagious enough for the Dickeys to shelve their misgivings about leaving their children at home. Like the rest of the happy group, they began to look forward to the trip.

In the boarding lounge with the high school group was New York-based architect Myriam Bellazoug, aged 30, who was returning to Paris to supervise the renovation of an apartment for the architectural firm of Peter Marino and Associates. She had worked in Paris some years earlier, but had returned to work in the United States in 1994. Three other architects/designers, all unrelated to each other, were en route to Paris that night. Jed Johnson, aged 47, of the firm Johnson/Wanzenberg and Associates, was a well-known designer for celebrity clients. His most famous client was the world-renowned artist Andy Warhol. Johnson was heading for Paris on a buying trip for his decorating firm. His partner of 15 years, Alan Wanzenberg, was staying behind in New York to run the business for Johnson while he was away.

Joan Benjamin, a freelance designer based in Bucks County, Pennsylvania, and Jill Watson, an architect from Pittsburgh, were also leaving for the designers' mecca of the world that evening.

On an entirely different kind of vacation were Dennis and Peggy Price. Dennis was the owner of a financial planning firm and Peggy, his wife, worked for United Airlines as a flight attendant. They were flying to Paris to start a two-week biking tour of France. Married in 1972 on a Friday the 13th, the Prices were everyone's idea of the ideal couple. Peggy's mother said that they were the kind of people who "didn't believe in anything bad," and so getting married on that unlucky day did not faze them at all.

Andrew Krukar was another passenger traveling for pleasure. The 40-year-old engineering manager was going to Paris to meet his fiancée, Julie Stuart, who was planning to join him the following week. He took on the plane a $15,000, 1.7-carat diamond ring he planned to give her when they met up in Paris. Also heading to the City of Lights, as Paris is called, were Gharran and Nina Haurani, in celebration of their 25th wedding anniversary.

Just beginning their married lives were Monica and Mirco Buttaroni, who after a three-week honeymoon were returning home to Italy. They were originally booked on Flight 848 to Rome, but since that flight was cancelled they were rescheduled for Flight 800 instead, and would catch a continuation flight from Paris. Monica and Mirco had just been married a month ago in their hometown of Lucrezia, Italy. Monica was working as a designer in her uncle's firm of J Cab in Fano, Italy, where she designed men's fashions for the international trade. Her new husband, Mirco, worked at a bank as an accountant. Four days after their wedding on June 23, the couple had boarded a plane for their honeymoon. It was the first time either of them had left home, and the first time either of them had flown in an airplane. They visited New York, Los Angeles, San Francisco, and the Dominican Republic before returning home.

During their honeymoon the couple had received bad news. Just a few days into the honeymoon, they called home only to find out that Mirco's grandmother, to whom he was very close, had died. The news was not unexpected, as she had been too ill to attend their wedding, but word of the death was still a shock for them both. Their first thoughts had been to end their honeymoon and return home early, but relatives convinced them to continue on and come back on the date originally planned. On July 17, both were anxious to get home to be with their loved ones.

Monica and Mirko Buttaroni were 2 of the 230 victims of the Flight 800 disaster. The couple had just been married and on July 17, 1996, were returning from their honeymoon in the United States to their home in Lucrezia, Italy.

Love was also in the air that evening when jazz musician Wayne Shorter received a call from Ana Maria, his wife of 26 years. She and Wayne's niece Dalila were traveling to meet him. Just before boarding the plane, Ana Maria called him. The two said "I love you" to each other during their brief conversation.

Other music-makers were taking the trip to Paris. Musician David Hogan was going to Paris to write music, and French musician Marcel Dadi was returning home with an award he had received for his work.

A small group of businessmen holding first-class tickets was also bound for Paris, where they hoped to close a business deal. Charles Henry Gray III was the chief operating officer of the Midland Financial Group. He, along with Kirk Rhein, hoped to find financing for a merger they were working on. Godi Notes, an Israeli-born American, was working for the investment firm that they hoped would assist Gray and the others in the merger, and William Story, president of the firm, was also to board Flight 800 that night.

Gray had originally been scheduled to be on a flight from Hartford to Dulles Airport in Washington, D.C., where he was booked on another flight to Paris, but his driver got lost on the way to the airport. Gray had to scramble to get on a flight to Paris, and ended up on the

TWA Flight 800 leaving from New York along with Rhein, Notes, and Story.

Another passenger was Susan Hill, a police detective from Oregon. A born-again Christian, Hill was a recent divorcée planning an extended vacation. She was taking a five-week trip, which would begin in Paris, where she would house-sit for the relative of a friend at her police station. Afterward she would continue touring in England. Her seatmate, Matthew Alexander, would have probably offered great conversation during the long flight. He was traveling to Dijon, France, where he planned to spend the summer doing Christian missionary work.

All the passengers who boarded TWA Flight 800 had assigned seats—except one. Max, a small terrier dog that belonged to Judith Yee, was allowed on the flight but had to be kept in his pet carrier, beneath the seat of his adoring owner. Max was a working dog, whose job took him with his owner once a week to P.S. 138, an elementary school located in Greenwich Village in New York City. During these visits, disabled students could interact with the dog. Max and another dog, a Labrador, became the center of attention at the school each week as the children would be encouraged and guided to touch, pet, and groom the animals.

Judith Yee was celebrating the end of the school year and had planned the trip to Paris, taking with her two friends, her cousin Patricia Loo from New Jersey and Angela Murta, a friend she had known for more than 20 years. The group was flying TWA because Yee had found out that it was the only airline that would allow Max to travel in the cabin instead of the cargo hold of the airplane.

All 230 passengers on TWA Flight 800 perished in one of the worst airline disasters in U.S. history. Some had planned months earlier to be on the flight; others had only ended up on it by some quirk of fate. However, there were also some passengers who were supposed to be on Flight 800 who had the good fortune to miss it.

Donna George, a flight attendant for TWA, was scheduled to work that night, but she had changed her plans because her son Eddie George had just been signed as the number one draft pick for the Houston Oilers, a professional football team. Signing this five-year contract meant that George, a Heisman Trophy winner, would get a $6.9 million deal from the Oilers, including a $2.9 signing bonus.

Even though Donna George knew of this lucrative deal for her son and wanted to be there when he accepted it, she initially did not want to change her work schedule to accompany him to the signing on July 19, in Houston. However, her son's agent, Lamont Smith, persisted and finally convinced her to change her schedule and cancel working the July 17th flight. After hearing about the crash, Smith said, "[The Georges] were already spiritual people, and they say the Lord works in mysterious ways. If He worked through me in this instance, I couldn't be happier about it." Eddie George said after the incident: "I thank God every day she didn't get on that plane. I know we've been blessed, and my prayers go out to the families of those who died."

After waiting past the original departure time of 7:00 P.M., the TWA Flight 800 passengers were starting to get annoyed. The first delay occurred because TWA cancelled the flight to Rome and had to combine it with the flight to Paris. This change also called for the airline to rearrange the flight crew, which also took up more time.

Due to an increase in number of terrorist threats, new security measures called for all airlines to match every piece of baggage placed on the plane to the passenger list. This had become a widely used security measure after the 1998

crash of a Pan Am Flight in Scotland following the explosion of a bomb on board. One piece of baggage on Flight 800 was unmatched, causing yet another delay as the TWA crew searched for the passenger who owned the bag.

Finally at 8:00 P.M., the new pilots and flight crew had everything in place and were ready for departure. After takeoff, the navigational path of TWA Flight 800 would take the plane over East Moriches, New York, before the craft attained a cruising altitude and headed out for the transatlantic crossing to Paris.

In all likelihood, none of the passengers or the crew had ever heard of East Moriches, New York. Neither did many other people until Flight 800's voyage to Paris was cut short at this exact location, making East Moriches, New York, its final destination.

During the 1996 tragedy there was one good story concerning TWA flight attendant Donna George (right). She was scheduled to work on the ill-fated flight to Paris, but decided at the last minute to cancel because her son, Eddie George (left), was being signed as a professional football player for the Houston Oilers.

East
Moriches

An aerial view of the U.S. Coast Guard station at East Moriches, New York. The peaceful, coastal town was the last place expected to serve as a site for a federal investigation into the TWA Flight 800 crash.

2

Just south of the Long Island Expressway, which runs through Long Island, New York, lies East Moriches. Until the night of July 17, 1996, it was a little-known Long Island community.

Many would consider East Moriches a sort of Norman Rockwell type of place to live. Lying far enough southeast of Manhattan to be undisturbed by the hustle and bustle of big-city life, East Moriches offers the quiet of a small-town community. It's also far enough away from the chic and trendy Hamptons to be unaffected by the high-society life found there. East Moriches residents are typically working-class families with old-time values. Most of the townspeople know each other, and it is a friendly place to live in.

Many of the town's inhabitants have their own boats, which they use for leisurely pursuits. As a seacoast town, East Moriches has a strong fishing trade. The people there respect the sea and know how to deal with its challenges.

The residents of East Moriches live a peaceful life—or at least they did until TWA Flight 800 crossed over its shoreline. The last thing anyone there expected was to be thrown into the international limelight on the night of July 17.

And the last thing anyone boarding the TWA Flight 800 to Paris ever expected was to have his or her life snuffed out just 12 short minutes after departure. All passengers were headed to the City of Light with great expectations of having a wonderful holiday or celebration of some kind. On that day, TWA was itself celebrating the 50th anniversary of its first transatlantic flight. Ironically enough, that flight in 1946 was also bound for Paris.

The plane that TWA scheduled to fly to Paris and then to Rome was a Boeing 747. People can easily recognize it for its hump at the front of the plane, formed as a result of the two-cabin configuration that early on became its trademark. When it first came into use, passengers liked the 747 for the spaciousness of the cabin. It's also known as the "jumbo jet," being able to transport up to 400 passengers. Recently, the major American airlines were using fewer 747s, and at the time of the Flight 800 crash some were using none at all. TWA would retire the last of its 747s in 1997.

On the evening of July 17, 1996, the Boeing 747 plane that would become known simply as Flight 800 had arrived after completing a trip that originated in Athens, Greece. The flight crew that brought the plane into John F. Kennedy International Airport had reported nothing unusual during the flight from Athens.

The Flight 800 plane had been manufactured by Boeing in 1971. Identified by Boeing as 747-131, it was the

153rd plane off the assembly line. TWA assigned the craft the tail number N93119, which the airline would use to keep track of the plane throughout its lifespan. TWA had received the plane from Boeing on October 27, 1971, and kept it for a little over four years. Then the company sold the plane back to Boeing in 1975, which planned to sell it to the Imperial Iran air force. But when the deal fell through, Boeing sold the craft back to TWA the following year.

During its 25 years of flying, the 747 had tallied up 16,000 flights and in the two weeks before its final trip as Flight 800 had clocked in 100,000 miles. The plane had an excellent safety record and in its long history, there were only 106 recorded mechanical problems. While it was in commission, the plane had had only two minor incidents. The first one was on May 11, 1987, when a tire blew during takeoff and damaged the landing gear; the second was on September 23, 1988, when pilots were forced to shut down one of the engines after noticing a low oil pressure reading. On the surface, there was certainly nothing to indicate that the plane's mechanical equipment was unreliable.

The only consistently reported complaint about the plane that would have some bearing on the crash later was a recurrent difficulty refueling the plane's wing tanks. Fuel technicians would make eight reports of this nature about plane number N93119. The final report was filed on the night of July 17, when the technicians had to override the automatic shutoff control system in order to fill the plane's wing tanks. However, the mechanics left the center tank empty, a decision that many people would later consider an ill-advised move.

There had also been nine separate reports of incorrect readings on the fuel flow gauge. Most reports of this nature are considered to be normal in the course of an airplane's maintenance history and not cause for alarm. Nor would the crews flying the plane be considered negligent for not knowing about the problem.

The practice of leaving the plane's center tank empty was considered normal procedure within the aviation industry because this aircraft did not need a full load of fuel when traveling from the United States to Europe. Taking on more fuel than necessary for its flight would make the plane heavier and thus more costly to fly.

The empty center fuel tank would become the cause for much speculation in the ensuing days and months of the crash investigations. The crew of TWA Flight 800 was not aware of the reported problems with the plane's fuel flow gauges. However, as the plane took off from Kennedy Airport, the cockpit crew did note that one of the engine's performance gauges was possibly malfunctioning. The problem seemed to have corrected itself almost immediately, however, and was not cause for much concern. Only after the crash would investigators look into the problem with gauges in the course of querying every possible cause for the disaster that befell Flight 800.

Another question surrounding that TWA Flight 800 bound for Paris was why it did not have its originally scheduled crew members. They had been replaced by 56-year-old Captain Steven Snyder and 58-year-old First Officer Captain Ralph Kevorkian, who along with flight engineers Oliver Krick and Richard Campbell were supposed to have crewed the cancelled TWA Flight 848 to Rome. Krick had almost completed his training to become a commercial airline pilot, needing just a few more hours of supervision to do so, and Captain Kevorkian was completing his last supervised flight.

With their flight cancelled, Kevorkian, Krick, Snyder, and Campbell were originally to travel on the flight to

Henry Snyder, brother of TWA pilot Steve Snyder, is comforted by a loved one at a memorial service held for the crash victim.

Paris as passengers. In the airline industry, this is known as "deadheading." If space is available on a plane, airline employees can fly for reduced fares or sometimes for free. The term "deadhead" refers to the spot in the head count that does not make the airline money but is nonetheless counted for safety reasons. Instead of letting them fly as deadheads, Snyder requested that Kevorkian and Krick be allowed to replace the original crew of Flight 800 so they could get more experience; the originally scheduled crew of Flight 800 could then deadhead in their place. TWA agreed to the arrangement, and so on the night of

Flight 800's departure, Oliver Krick and Captain Ralph Kevorkian found themselves in front of the controls.

The flight crew began the time-consuming process of making sure that all systems were in order and began its preflight checklist for the scheduled 7:00 P.M. departure. Of the 230 people on board the flight, only 176 were paying passengers. The remaining 54 passengers were airline employees, some with family members who were taking advantage of airline policy, which allowed them to fly for free—space permitting. Since the 747 can carry a full load of 433, there was no shortage of seats available that evening.

As the pilots continued their preflight checks and preparations, the crew began to assist passengers in boarding the plane. When the pilots and crew were ready to leave, however, there was the hold-up because the computers were having difficulty matching the piece of luggage to one of the passengers. It would take an hour before the baggage would be matched to the passenger and the pilots could announce that Flight 800 was ready for departure. But then, they had to state there was yet another delay due to bad weather in Chicago and that the plane had to wait for passengers connecting to the flight from Chicago's O'Hare Airport.

In total, the plane had been on the ground for three hours. During this time the aircraft's air conditioning machines had been left running, which is standard procedure during delays. Like the fuel gauges, the air conditioners would be one more detail that would later spark questions about the cause of the crash.

Flight 800 was getting ready to move down the tarmac and heading for takeoff at 8:00 P.M., and nothing seemed amiss. It took off without any difficulties and was airborne within minutes, flying out into the clear night sky. There was no reason to anticipate trouble of any kind.

TWA pilot Ralph Kevorkian was behind the controls on TWA Flight 800 while pilot Steve Snyder observed his performance. The flight to Paris would have been Kevorkian's last supervised flight before he became a full-fledged captain.

Nobody had any reason to doubt the flight would not make it to Paris.

Yet, just 12 minutes after takeoff, with no warning of any kind, the huge airliner of Flight 800 tumbled into the sea in bits and pieces. Impossible as it was to imagine, a plane with an excellent safety record, and an experienced crew flying it, plunged into the ocean, ripped apart by an enormous explosion. As the plane broke apart, fuel from the ruptured wing tanks created a huge fireball, visible to witnesses from miles around. This fireball, described by many, would also be the cause of much investigation and speculation in the weeks and months after the crash.

One of the first people to spot the disturbance in the sky and connect it with Flight 800 was pilot David McClain. Flying about ten miles behind Flight 800 in a Boeing 737 with Vincent Fuschetti at the helm, McClain observed something wrong with the plane in front of them. Before he could register what it was, the plane exploded in front of his eyes.

McClain quickly called air traffic control in Boston to report the blast. "Ah, we just saw an explosion up ahead of us here, somewhere about sixteen thousand feet or something like that," he said. "It just went down . . . into the water." The Boston air controller tried for several minutes to raise Flight 800 on the radio, but there was no response. McClain broke the silence, telling the controller, "I think that was him." The controller agreed. "God bless him," said McClain.

Another pilot, Senior Navy NCO Dwight Brumley, was on U.S. Air Flight 217 when he noticed something in the sky. Brumley's account is more complete with details. He was in a window seat near the front of the plane when he said he saw a bright object pass parallel to his plane. A 25-year navy veteran with some experience with missiles, he thought that the bright object was a missile, but that it was past the launch phase. Moments later he saw an explosion in the sky.

Bill Gallagher, a commercial fisherman, saw much the same thing. He was about ten miles away from Flight 800 and claimed to have seen a bright flare hit the belly of the plane.

Shaun Brady and Jake Johnson, two parachutists from the 106th Rescue Wing of the New York Air National Guard, had just finished jumping from their C-130 transport plane when they reported seeing a giant fireball light up the sky. Fearing that it came from the C-130 that they just jumped from, they radioed their plane. Major Mike Weiss, the C-130 pilot, responded: "Negative, It's not us. We see the fire as well. . . . We're heading to find it."

National Guard pilot Captain Christian Baur was flying in a Sikorsky Pave Hawk helicopter when he spotted a white flash in the sky. He thought at first that it might have been flares being tossed from the C-130 transport plane as part of its practice run. Before he could question it further, though, the night sky lit up as if on fire. He then heard the pilot of the C-130 on the radio to the control tower saying, "Notify the Coast Guard. It looks like two planes have collided. We're heading over."

The helicopter and the transport plane both headed to where they'd seen the ball of fire fall into the ocean only to realize that they were dangerously close to the falling debris. After identifying pieces of a tail section, they quickly gathered that the parts were the remains of an exploded plane. As the men watched, the massive oil slick on the water ignited. Then they spotted the inflatable evacuation slides and realized that the plane must have been a downed passenger jet. They began to circle the area, hoping to find survivors. Weiss radioed the control tower. "This has to be a passenger jetliner," he said. "Call the authorities." The first question that control asked was if there were survivors, but Weiss had to tell them that there was none from what he could see.

Brady and Johnson disregarded this grim prediction. After finishing their jump they quickly gathered emergency medical equipment from the 106th Rescue Wing station and headed out to the site in a helicopter. Optimistic that there would be survivors to rescue, Brady and Johnson cleared away space in the chopper before rushing out to the scene.

Dozens of eyewitnesses, including pilot and missile expert Dwight Brumley, reported seeing a bright light flying toward the plane before the explosion. Their testimony led many to believe a missile had caused the disaster.

In the water near the crash site, two members of the Coast Guard, Jarrl Pellinen and Ken Seebeck, were just coming in from towing a sailboat to shore. Just as they were returning to their boat, the *Monarch*, a petty officer named Rick Freese told them he had received a call for them to quickly return to East Moriches. When they boarded the *Monarch*, they heard distress calls reporting explosions, emergency flares, and falling debris in an area not far from their own Coast Guard station.

Once aboard, Pellinen and Seebeck called the station

back to get more details of what to expect when they arrived at the site and how they should prepare themselves. Freese said, "The cutter *Adak* is there and they will be in command. It appears to be a commercial airliner in the water." He added, "There are numerous people in the water." Seebeck and Pellinen also hoped to find survivors and got out their emergency medical kits.

Both Coast Guard ships proceeded to search the site for survivors. At one point the *Monarch* got so close that its motors became tangled up in some of the wreckage. Requesting help from the *Adak*, the *Monarch*'s crew managed to disengage itself at the last minute and was able to get safely away before the flames near the site consumed it.

Eyewitnesses to the explosion were many, and with very similar stories, they gave a strong collective account. One man who had fishing nearby explained, "It started off like a little ball, like a flare. It came down for a few seconds and all of a sudden burst into flames, a big ball of flame." Another eyewitness told a nearly identical story: "I saw a big fireball with pieces coming off of it. I heard two big explosions, like two big firecrackers going off."

Immediately following the disaster, and in the years that would follow, these eyewitness accounts would serve to support the first theory that Flight 800 was brought down by a missile attack. The second theory was that a terrorist attack caused the crash, and the third was that the plane had a massive mechanical failure. The tragedy and mystery surrounding TWA Flight 800 had just begun.

First on the Scene and First Reports

3

From the moment that Flight 800 plunged into the sea, a prearranged set of plans went into motion. Two separate teams of investigators typically handle aircraft disasters. The National Transportation Safety Board (NTSB) sends out one team, and its members function as technical specialists trying to determine the cause of the accident. The Federal Bureau of Investigation (FBI) and other police agencies send the second team. Both work side-by-side to try to determine any and all possible causes for a disaster like the Flight 800 explosion.

The person heading up the FBI part of the investigation was deputy director James Kallstrom, chief of the New York division. He had been notified about the crash after his pager went off as he was leaving a dinner honoring Raymond Kelly, a former New York City police commissioner. He immediately called the FBI duty officer to find out what he was being paged for. At the same time that Kallestrom was holding this conversation, his wife was receiving a phone call at home from their longtime friend Charles Christopher, another FBI agent. Christopher's wife, Janet, was a TWA flight attendant and he was calling to tell Kallstrom's wife that she was on Flight 800. "Janet's plane has gone down," he told her. "It's crashed. I need Jim. We've got to find her."

Within the week, Kallstrom, heading the FBI's team, would assemble no fewer than 300 agents to determine the cause of the disaster that had taken the life of his friend, along with 229 others. His team started working 20-hour days between their command post in the city and at the crash site in East Moriches. Initially believing that the explosion was the result of a terrorist attack, Kallstrom had declared, "If this is a terrorist attack, there is absolutely no doubt in my mind that we will know who did this and where they are. The only question is, can we take them around the neck?"

The NTSB team was headed by chairman Jim Hall, who along with Peter Goelz, the public information officer for the NTSB, and Robert Francis, the board's vice chairman, received the news about Flight 800 at about the same time. Hall and Goelz were on their way to a movie with their wives when they heard the first report, which was sketchy at best. Both men rushed to headquarters to find transportation to the scene. Their first thought was that a mechanical failure had caused the disaster.

The media had picked up on the story almost immediately. Ed Block, an aircraft wiring expert for the Pentagon, was watching the news that night and what he heard was unsettling, confirming fears he had had for years. From 1974 to 1984, Block had been in charge of purchasing aircraft wiring for military planes, and had developed a firm understanding of the electrical systems of planes. By 1981,

he had become convinced that substandard wiring was causing several navy fighter jet accidents. Block had determined that 20 percent of 600 F-14 accidents had occurred because of some sort of electrical trouble.

This conclusion had come after Block spent years researching problems with wiring materials. As early as 1978, Block's office, the Defense Industrial Supply Center, had been instructed to remove a wiring product called Poly-X, manufactured by Raychem. The military had been using this product and over the years it had become evident that the insulation of this particular material was breaking down. The resulting corrosion would allow electricity into areas, potentially creating heat or fire, or sending false

James Kallstrom (left), director of the Federal Bureau of Investigation's New York office, would become one of the most important figures in the investigation of the plane crash. Here, Kallstrom sits with FBI director Louis Freeh at a memorial mass for flight victims.

electric signals to flight controls. This same material was being used in many 747 commercial airliners.

In 1992, Block had written a letter to the General Accounting Office, where he worked, asking experts at the Federal Aviation Administration (FAA) and the NTSB to run tests to ascertain what part faulty or substandard wiring could be playing in aviation accidents. As often happens in large bureaucracies, Block received a reply but no action was taken. One month before the crash of Flight 800, he had sent yet another letter to the FAA about the wiring problems that he suspected were playing a large part in aviation crashes—both military and commercial. In his letter to Tom McSweeny, FAA director of aircraft certification, he referred to an earlier airline accident resulting from an aging aircraft: "Just as it took an Aloha Airlines 737 to flip its lid to focus attention on metal fatigue, similarly wire and cable has virtually been ignored."

Ironically, the dismissive reply to this letter came a month after the crash of Flight 800: "The FAA has no plans to update or make any changes to its wire performance standards. This is partly due to the fact that the wiring industry is providing outstanding products to the airframers." It would take more than a year of investigating the crash of Flight 800 before McSweeny would agree to work with Block and investigate the possibility that faulty wiring could be affecting airline safety.

The media was pressed to come to quick conclusions about what had caused the massive jetliner to fall from the sky. The first report of the crash of Flight 800 in East Moriches, New York, oddly enough came to the attention of an Associated Press writer in Phoenix, Arizona. Michelle Boorstein was in Arizona when she had heard a vague ABC news report about "some kind of explosion— possibly a plane crash—off Long Island." Supervisor

SLOW MOTION
1/4-SCALE TEST WITH JET FUEL AND SIMULATED VAPOR

THOMAS MCSWEENY   IVOR TH

John Rogers called the Associated Press (AP) general desk in New York to report the story and found that the New York bureau's supervisor had already heard, having received the news from a tip service that monitors police scanners.

The AP still had to check out the story with the FAA to confirm that a plane crash had actually taken place. But the news agency quickly rushed to send out a short story indicating that the Coast Guard had reported an explosion in the Atlantic Ocean off Long Island and that every available cutter was being sent to the scene. The last paragraph of the article stated that authorities did not believe the incident to be a plane crash. This blunder was based on the police sources, which indicated that

Many officials including Thomas McSweeny, director of aircraft certification for the Federal Aviation Administration, would be slow to attribute the 1996 air disaster to a mechanical failure. Here, McSweeny testifies at a 1997 hearing about the problems with TWA Flight 800's fuel tank.

airport control towers in New York had received no reports of a missing plane. The story was entitled simply "AM-Long Island Explosion."

It was only later that the AP found out that the airport control towers in New York did not have any record of "missing" planes because Flight 800's pilots had, according to procedure, switched over to Boston's radar system after take-off. New York's radar tracking devices had not recorded the explosion, but Boston's devices had.

The vague story began to take on a life of its own as reporters scurried to get more information from whatever sources they could. It wasn't long before they learned that the "explosion" was a plane crash and that the plane was TWA Flight 800. Reports of the disaster started to pour in from many sources. Soon eyewitnesses were doing television interviews, giving accounts of a huge fireball they had seen in the sky. The Coast Guard announced that there appeared to be no survivors. Their grim accounts of plane wreckage burning in the water and of body parts of the victims being brought to shore made it clear that this was a story to which the media would give much attention.

As news agencies jumped into the fray, reports became more and more explicit as to what might have caused this disaster. In Atlanta, where the Olympic games were due to begin in two days, the news reporters and Olympic personnel were worried. If Flight 800 had been the victim of a successful terrorist attack, then the Atlanta games might be the next target. Authorities in Atlanta had tightened security already in preparation for the Olympics, but they now planned to beef up safety measures even more.

The AP International Desk in Paris sent a correspondent to the airport, but initially nobody there knew much. Frightened relatives waiting for passengers arriving on

Flight 800 could only worry and try to understand the sign posted on the flight information monitor that simply read, "cancelled."

Meanwhile Patrice Soualle, the station manager for TWA at Charles de Gaulle Airport was awakened to the call that everyone in the aviation business dreads. He was informed that Flight 800 had crashed with no survivors. Within 15 minutes Soualle was on his way to the airport to implement TWA's emergency plan. He knew that the families of the passengers on Flight 800 would soon be arriving at the airport. "Focus on the mission. Handle the families, attend to their needs," Soualle told himself. "There's nothing else you can do."

The initial confusion that surrounded the first reports of what had happened in East Moriches, New York, was only to get worse as the investigation of the crash flew into high gear.

Security officials at the 1996 Summer Olympics in Atlanta, Georgia, were especially cautious after experts suspected that a terrorist attack caused the Flight 800 disaster. Here, a soldier searches a truck driver about to enter the Olympic area.

At 8:50 P.M. on July 17, the Emergency Net News (ENN) sent out the following flash report:

ENN is receiving preliminary reports regarding the "explosion" and crash of a TWA 747, Flight #800, en route to Paris, France, from Kennedy Airport. It is believed to be in the water approximately 10 miles south of Moriches Bay in Suffolk County, NY. A major sea rescue is underway, including 6 Coast Guard Helicopters and Coast Guard Cutters. Private craft are also assisting in the rescue. As many as 229 souls were believed to be on-board the ill-fated flight. Bodies of victims are being seen in the water and reported by marine radio. Requests are going out for additional assistance. ENN is gathering more information from the scene and will provide it as soon as possible. Speculation is centering on a "major explosion" and/or possible terrorist attack.

Some of the first people to arrive at the site where Flight 800 went down were the residents of East Moriches. Those same people who used their boats primarily for family outings now raced to sea as part of the recovery operation. Most hoped to find and rescue any survivors. Coast Guard cutters soon followed, many manned by citizens just 18 and 19 years old. As they came upon bodies in the water, they would call into their radios for help. Within a very short period of time, the police and emergency cars arrived at the East Moriches shore. The media had caught wind of the story and a local TV station grimly advised its listeners, "If anyone should find a body part on shore, call 911."

The initial hope that people would find survivors to bring to safety soon expired, as it was obvious that there would be none. One of the East Moriches residents said, "When my neighbor and I headed out in his Whaler, we thought we were going to find survivors. We came upon dead bodies, but we kept looking for people who were still alive. Then we realized nobody was alive. I saw legs, a head. I said, 'Please, God, don't let me see a kid.' Then I saw a kid."

One of the first townsperson to reach the crash site was a man in his fifties. He and a friend had rushed out in their boat hoping to find survivors to rescue. "We saw floating bodies, two or three," he said. "But we let them pass. We were looking for the living. After awhile, we knew that nobody had made it, so we started pulling up the dead."

In spite of the enormous efforts, a day after the crash only 100 bodies had been recovered. The town of East Moriches found itself being cordoned off by the National Guard and the Coast Guard. Residents understandably reacted with shock to what had happened. And although they lived in the site where the plane came down, most received news of what was happening from television reports. One resident who had hoped to find people alive in the water said, "I can't stop talking about it. My friend who was with me can't sleep. And I can't stop talking."

In order to help investigators examine the crash site, most of the people from East Moriches were asked to leave debris that washed up on the beaches untouched and to just mark what they found. Roger Rosenblatt, a writer and visitor to the area, recalls walking the beach in the aftermath of the tragedy and finding many of these marked items along the shoreline. The coastline already contained various items that had washed ashore after tropical storm Bertha, which had struck the previous week, but what Rosenblatt found must have come from the downed plane. There were items like serving trays, a one-size-fits-all baseball cap, and an imitation alligator eyeglass case.

Residents and visitors continued to stroll the beaches and streets of East Moriches in a stunned grim silence.

Where to Begin

It wasn't until more than three hours after the crash that TWA made its first public announcement about Flight 800. Mike Kelly, vice president of airport operations, would have the difficult task of facing the press in New York. The person who should have made the announcement was TWA's director of media relations, John McDonald, who was in St. Louis when the tragedy occurred. He had received thousands of messages from reporters about the crash and knew that the airline had to make an official statement. TWA's policy mandates this kind of announcement come from the top-ranking officer within the corporate structure, but McDonald was unable to get to New York fast enough.

After McDonald, the next two officials in line to make a public statement were TWA's vice president for corporate communications, Mark Abels, and

TWA's chief executive officer, Jeffrey Erickson. But both of those men were in London, where they were working on a successful bid to resume flights to and from London's Heathrow Airport and gain more business for TWA.

Kelly was in a terrible predicament: he not only had to deal with a terrible tragedy, but he also was handicapped with insufficient information to tell the press. McDonald had only advised him to "stick to the facts." Of much concern to anyone connected with TWA was whether or not the airline itself could be blamed for the crash. At that time, there was such little information about why the plane had crashed that there was plenty reason to worry. So in his official statement, Kelly did stick to the facts, although all he could and would say was that Flight 800 had gone down off the southern coast of Long Island. He added that rescue efforts manned by Coast Guard Air Sea Rescue vehicles and Suffolk County authorities, with the assistance of private boat owners, were at the site to search for possible survivors, but that "there were no estimates on the number of possible survivors." After Kelly made his brief public announcement to the press, which had assembled at Kennedy Airport, he was asked to wait for the arrival of New York City mayor Rudolph Guiliani.

When Guiliani arrived, Kelly informed him that TWA had little information beyond the facts: a plane flight bound for Paris, with approximately 200 people on board, had disappeared from radar. Mayor Guiliani responded by directing his attention toward the families of the passengers on Flight 800.

Two employees of TWA, Mary Anne Kelly and Jamie Hogan, were on hand at the New York City airport, trying to help the family members of Flight 800 passengers settle into JFK's Ambassador Club lounge. Just as this was being accomplished, George Marlin, the head of the

Port Authority of New York, appeared and requested a complete manifest, a list of the flight's passengers. As chief officer for the Port Authority, the agency responsible for operations at the three major airports in New York and New Jersey, Marlin was responsible for obtaining this information from TWA. However, TWA was unable to provide the manifest to Marlin at that time.

Meanwhile, it was becoming evident that the families and friends of the passengers on Flight 800 were going to be involved in a media circus. In order to shield them from this unneeded attention, emergency workers arranged for the group to go to the Ramada Inn Hotel near the airport, where they would be given information as soon as it became available. Of tantamount importance to everyone was determining whether their friends and relatives were indeed on that flight.

Arrangements were made for a bus from the Port Authority to transport family members to the hotel. But before it arrived, the camera crews and press had arrived. Now frightened and worried relatives had to cope with reporters asking them questions they didn't have the answers to yet.

As the families of victims of Flight 800 headed to the Ramada Inn at John F. Kennedy Airport in New York, a TWA St. Louis–based trauma team was rushing there to assist them. Johanna O'Flaherty headed the group of 675 volunteers, who had to overcome their own initial shock. After all, among the 230 passengers lost on Flight 800 were 54 fellow TWA employees. Eighteen had made up the working crew that night; the rest had been taking advantage of employee flight benefits and heading off for vacations in Paris or Rome.

About four hours after Mike Kelly's press conference, TWA's vice president of operations, Rich Roberts, arrived at JFK airport from Washington, D.C. Roberts knew little about what had happed other than what the press had been told, but he knew that any kind of rescue operation was going to be hampered by the dark of night. Perhaps because he was focusing on the details of the crash and the airline's possible role in it, Roberts did not supply Mayor Guiliani with the passenger list that he'd requested. The resulting delay in officially notifying the families about who had died in the crash caused much heartache, and it created a huge rift between TWA and the mayor, who had become a representative for the victims' families.

Meanwhile Jim Hall, the chairman of the National Transportation Safety Board, had learned that the 747 had gone down off the coast of Long Island and that a search and rescue operation had been mounted. He was aware that the chances for any survivors didn't look good; all other details remained sketchy.

Hall was no stranger to disaster, given the nature of his job, and his way of dealing with tragedy differed from others' approaches. Since 1995, when he had been called in to investigate the crash of a U.S. Air plane, Hall had become increasingly concerned at how the airlines handled the delicate matter of dealing with the families of the victims. That year he had decided to make it a policy to meet with family members and keep them informed about what was happening, instead of keeping information about the investigation separate from them. Hall argued, "If we are not doing these investigations for the family members, who in the hell are we doing them for?"

Detractors of Hall's hands-on approach to dealing with victims' families believed that the purpose of the NTSB clearly was not to worry about the families, but instead to investigate and work towards preventing the disasters that produce victims in the first place.

Before even facing this particular dilemma, Hall would run into problems getting his team promptly to

New York. He wanted a team from the NTSB, based in Washington, D.C., to travel to New York immediately. The government keeps a private plane on hand for the use of the NTSB, but although the plane was ready to fly, the agency had failed to have a flight crew scheduled to fly it. Since pilots follow strict sleep time regulations, it is not always easy to find a flight crew on short notice. Peter Goelz, the NTSB public information officer, was appalled and demanded, "What's the point of having a plane on standby for the NSTB if there's no one standing by to fly [it]?"

Investigating the disaster and handling the relatives of

National Transportation Safety Board president Robert Francis addresses the media after meeting with relatives of TWA Flight 800 victims. From early on in the investigation, the NTSB maintained that the crash was due to a mechanical failure.

the Flight 800 victims were difficult tasks made even harder by the media frenzy that grew out of the disaster. One callous reporter for the *New York Post,* Tonice Sgrignoli, went so far as to successfully impersonate a relative of a victim. She gained access to the Ramada Hotel where the emergency staff sequestered the victims' families specifically to shield them from the press.

Sgrignoli claimed to be a cousin of a Flight 800 passenger, and was so successful at this impersonation that she even went to memorial services for victims of the crash. Eventually, she realized that since she would later have to reveal herself as an impersonator upon writing the story, she might as well give the act up and go home. In order to leave the premises, she revealed her true identity to one of the assigned escorts, who quickly turned her in. She was then led away from the hotel in handcuffs.

Tonice Sgrignoli faced five felony charges, including criminal trespass, criminal impersonation, and possession of stolen property. She was issued the stolen property charge for falsely obtaining one of the lapel buttons that were issued to the relatives of victims for admittance into the Ramada Hotel. Months later when her case finally came to trial, the court ordered her to write a letter of apology to a woman whom she had befriended during her stay at the Ramada, and the *New York Post* had to pay a fine. When she returned to work at the *New York Post* she was greeted with a hero's welcome.

Other journalists were not so kind about Sgrignoli's methods of obtaining a story and felt that ploys like hers made the profession seem dishonest and unethical. Many responsible journalists had taken great pains to dismantle the profession's bad reputation. As Suzanne Braun Levine, editor of the *Columbia Journalism Review*, told a *Newsweek* reporter, "You cannot set yourself up as a seeker of the truth and then behave as a purveyor of lies."

Reporters were not the only imposters to suddenly appear at the scene of the tragedy and surreptitiously gain access to secure areas. On the night of the crash, a well-dressed man in military uniform presented himself at the Coast Guard station in East Moriches. His military insignia identified him as a lieutenant colonel, and he said he was there to offer his help.

With so many planes and ships hurriedly being brought into the area to assist in the rescue mission, the Coast Guard needed every available hand, and the staff was glad for the assistance of the newcomer, who called himself David Williams. Had the scene not been so chaotic, in all likelihood someone might have noticed that although the man was wearing the traditional air force flight suit, his insignias were army issue. Because of the confusion and the fact that he seemed to know what he was doing, Williams managed to stay at the Coast Guard station, where he assisted with the landing of many helicopters during the three days that he was there.

Several pilots who had landed their planes according to Williams's directions thought that his methods were a bit unsafe, but since he was such a high-ranking officer, none of them suspected him. It wasn't until Williams's third day there that Colonel Frank Intini of the Army Aviation group noticed the discrepancies between the uniform and the insignias and questioned him. Williams was asked to leave the grounds immediately. His impersonation did not result in any gain for himself, and to this day it remains a mystery as to why he presented himself and offered his services at the Coast Guard station.

The people like Sgrignoli and Williams who had no legitimate business at all with Flight 800 only made the situation more chaotic for the other people with proper credentials who were needed. Amidst the confusion, one of the tasks that was not being completed was notifying the families of the disaster victims. It wasn't until the morning after the crash that the National Transportation Safety Board got word that TWA had confirmed the passenger list. Finally, after receiving the list, the TWA trauma team could spring into action and begin the arduous and tragic task of informing the next-of-kin.

Notification took almost an entire day to accomplish, and during the whole process the team was under pressure from the mayor. Because the families of the victims of Flight 800 were in Europe and the United States, the task was a lengthy one, which they also had to finish before there were any leaks to the media about the names of the flight's passengers. As it turned out, the last family of a victim was notified just 44 minutes before the passenger list was released to the press.

Johanna O'Flaherty, the director of the trauma team, was a seasoned member of the TWA crisis team. A native of Ireland, she'd begun working as a stewardess with Pan Am in 1970 while she also took classes and eventually earned a master's degree in clinical psychology. By this point, she became more interested in counseling than flying. In 1988, she'd been part of the team that helped victims' families after the bombing of Pan Am 103 over Lockerbie, Scotland. Later in 1995, TWA sent her and other fellow employees to Washington, D.C., to be trained by Michael Spinello, the deputy chief of staff of Army personnel.

TWA received a lot of criticism during the time of the disaster, but it is interesting that of the many airlines invited to the 1995 training session, TWA was the only one that chose to attend. During the course, Spinello shared with the TWA employees his personal experiences in dealing with major disasters, including notifying the loved ones of victims and other difficult duties that arise in the aftermath of a calamity. Every airline hopes that it

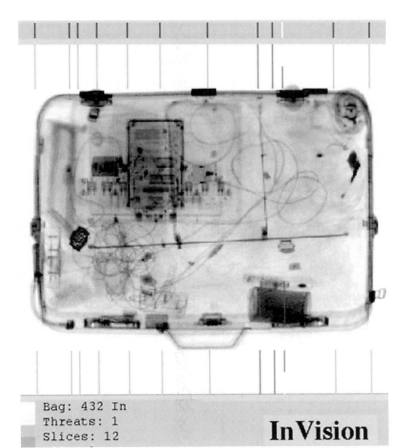

Bag: 432 In
Threats: 1
Slices: 12

InVision

An X-ray picture of a can bomb taken by the CTX-5000, which John F. Kennedy airport did not have installed at the time of the crash. Some proponents of the bomb theory argued that an explosive such as this one, made from unconventional materials, might have made it aboard Flight 800.

will never have to deal with such issues, but O'Flaherty, with her counseling background, wanted to be prepared just in case. Since then, she had become known within the TWA circle as the "Disaster Queen."

O'Flaherty's job was to prepare a team that could be ready to deal with the needs of survivors—not to notify the next-of-kin. That difficult task, according to airline protocol, falls to the airline's reservations division. Nevertheless, she was the first TWA executive to arrive at the Ramada Inn at John F. Kennedy Airport, and so she began to dispatch orders to the volunteers immediately.

A day after the crash, New York governor George Pataki went to East Moriches and spoke with reporters.

James Kallstrom, head of the FBI investigation, believed early on that a terrorist bomb had brought down Flight 800. Here, at a press conference he re-creates the flight scenario with a model of the 747.

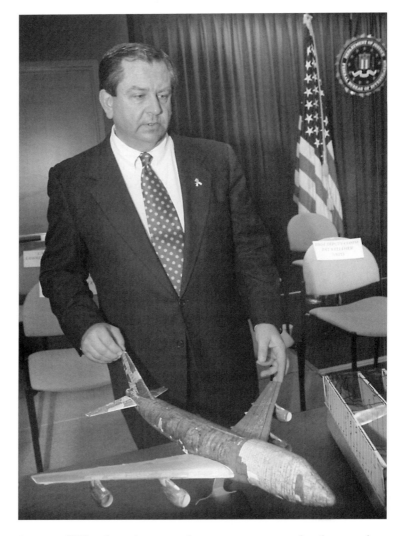

It was difficult to know what to say to people about what had happened to cause Flight 800 to plunge into the sea. Joining Pataki to speak with reporters were the director of the FBI's New York branch, James Kallstrom; Suffolk County medical examiner Charles Welti; and NTSB vice chairman Robert Francis.

Kallstrom had already told FBI director Louis Freeh all that he knew about what had happened, which at that time was not much. Due to the recent terrorist attacks taking place throughout the world, it was immediately assumed that terrorists had caused this disaster. The FBI began its investigation of the crash assuming that the incident was the criminal destruction of an aircraft.

At first, Kallstrom believed that a bomb brought down Flight 800, and would refute his position only later on. He defended his original theory by saying that the FBI had "made that assumption based on what we knew. First the plane blew up. We had almost instantaneous reports from other airplane crews. There was no communication from the cockpit, there was no distress call. And this business of people reporting that they'd seen things streaking in the sky, just those facts alone were enough."

Meanwhile, the NTSB continued to investigate the crash, believing the cause would prove to be mechanical failure. In the first days after the crash, though, all the NTSB could tell the public was that it would be a long time before any definitive analysis could be made.

One group of people believed that a missile brought down Flight 800 and that a massive cover-up was behind the subsequent investigation. Former White House press secretary Pierre Salinger, here holding a press conference in Paris, was one of the theory's biggest supporters.

The Theories

5

The NTSB's announcement that it would take time to get definite answers did nothing to stop the public's speculation about what had happened to Flight 800. Early in the investigation, three theories developed about the Flight 800 disaster. The first was the most logical and expected one—some sort of mechanical malfunction had caused the crash. The second theory was that the plane had been shot down by a missile, and a third was that, like the 1988 Pan Am Flight 103 disaster in Lockerbie, Scotland, TWA Flight 800 had been the target of a terrorist bombing. All three theories initially had some credence, and it would be months before investigators could be expected to determine which one was correct. The media frenzy and well-publicized speculations made it all the more difficult to conduct the investigations.

President Bill Clinton met with reporters two days after the crash and told them that the government was doing its best to recover the victims and the aircraft and to find the cause of the accident. He made the following statement:

> On behalf of the American people, I'd like to say to the families of the passengers of Flight 800, we are well aware that only the passage of time, the love of your family, and faith in God can ease your pain, but America stands with you. . . . Our government is doing everything we can to continue the search for survivors and to find the causes of the accident. . . . We will determine what happened. But for now, I want to caution again the American people against jumping to any conclusions and ask that today, overwhelmingly, our people remember the families of the people who are on the flight in their prayers.

However, the president's call to be patient apparently fell on deaf ears. From the moment Flight 800 went down, each of the three theories about what happened continued to gather momentum. The bomb, the missile, and the mechanical failure theories all had strong supporters who claimed to have their own proof explaining how and why Flight 800 crashed into the sea.

Those who believed that Flight 800 was shot down by a missile pointed to the eyewitness accounts of a bright flare-like object flying in the vicinity of the crash. If in fact the object was a missile, the military would be a prime suspect of friendly fire. The friendly fire theory gained most of its publicity through two individuals: James Sanders, a former Los Angeles police officer and author of *The Downing of TWA Flight 800*, and Pierre Salinger, a former White House press secretary.

Sanders paid close attention to a military zone known

as W-105, lying southeast of Moriches Inlet near East Moriches. The existence of the zone is not top secret information, and several locations in the immediate area, including a section of the sea, are also designated for military exercises. What the general public did not know, Sanders claimed, was that on the night of July 17, Area W-105 had just been activated by the United States Navy. The navy was purportedly testing the upgrade of its top-secret systems software and radar and its standard antiaircraft/antimissile system.

Sanders asserted that on July 17, in order to test the tracking capabilities of its radar systems, the U.S. Navy was engaged in a complicated military maneuver. Involved in this operation were helicopters, navy planes,

President Clinton addressed the nation on July 19 about the Flight 800 catastrophe, stating that the government was doing its best to recover any survivors. He also urged Americans not to jump to any conclusions about the cause of the disaster.

a Coast Guard cutter, and a submarine. The probable objective of this mission was to establish whether the missile's radar tracking devices—which the navy had been working on for three long years—were all it hoped they would be.

Since Area W-105 spans across land and sea and was located near John F. Kennedy International Airport, it would provide the navy with the exact conditions it needed to test its systems. In this area, navy supervisors have the opportunity to observe how the radar system would work in the presence of friendly, neutral, and hostile traffic. Theoretically, it is easy to designate the commercial air traffic as neutral or friendly on the navy's radar screens, thus simulating wartime conditions under which the system would have to operate.

The U.S. military would understandably be very anxious to get this kind of expertise fine-tuned. If the instruments worked the way that it hoped, the United States could have an edge on its rival nations. There has always been difficulty trying to determine solely by radar who is friendly, who is hostile, and who is neutral. With this newly upgraded and highly sophisticated software, Sanders explained, the military hoped to prove that it could accomplish this electronic miracle.

The crux of this military procedure's success would depend on the navy's new integrated radar system known as Cooperative Engagement Capability (CEC). This system was being controlled from a command post named Force 21, located in Fort Monmouth, New Jersey, under the direction of a senior naval officer, Admiral Edward K. Kristensen.

According to Sanders, on the night of July 17 the navy planned to send out a missile and a "hostile" target drone. With its new radar equipment the military planned to detect the drone and eliminate it with the missile.

Along with claiming inside information about the procedure, Sanders also said that he had access to physical evidence from the wreckage to support his missile theory. He had obtained "a mysterious reddish-orange residue" that would be irrefutable proof that a missile shot down the plane.

Sanders believed that what transpired that night was a huge military fiasco, and that TWA Flight 800 was mistaken for the hostile navy drone and shot down by the missile. According to Sanders, the CEC system was shut down momentarily by electronic interference, which could have thrown off the guidance on the missile. Sanders also claimed that those few seconds that the CEC was shut down corresponded exactly to the time that Flight 800 took off from John F. Kennedy International Airport, placing the plane precisely over Area W-105's airspace. Naval officers could have lost contact with the missile and the hostile drone while the missile proceeded to search the area for a target. During that few seconds of time that elapsed before it went back on track, the missile could have inadvertently already locked onto TWA Flight 800 and identified it as its target instead of the drone.

Sanders asserted that before navy officers could manually alter the missile's electronic course, the missile went straight for Flight 800, hitting it in front of the right wing. The impact caused the plane to start to break apart, which created a fire in the center fuel tank. The plane then went down in pieces.

Sanders's missile theory had an immediate following. David Hendrix, a writer for the *Press-Enterprise* in Riverside, California, and Christina Borjesson, a freelance producer for CBS, both pursued his claim. Like Sanders, Hendrix believed that a massive government cover-up was leading the public away from the real cause of the crash. Hendrix based his argument on some irrefutable navy documentation he had received that indicated specifically what exercises were being held on the night of July 17. The documentation proved that the *Normandy*, a guided missile cruiser, along with other submarines, were in the area that night. The navy told Hendrix that there were no submarines in the area, but he became suspicious and believed that he and other reporters were on what he called a "trail of misinformation." He said, "The media seems afraid that it will find out that the plane was hit by friendly fire."

Sanders's missile theory would get the most attention when former ABC news correspondent and White House press secretary Pierre Salinger stepped forward with supposed evidence of his own. Salinger said that he had heard the testimony from eyewitnesses who saw a bright light heading toward the plane just before it exploded. He also based his claim on a radar tape he had seen that showed a distinct "blip" heading toward the plane. In March 1997, Salinger stated conclusively that he believed that "the plane was unfortunately and mistakenly shot down by a naval missile."

Was this scenario believable? It was possible, given that there seemed to be a great deal of factual evidence to bolster the claim made by Salinger, Sanders, and others. However, the conspiracy case was dealt a great blow when the missile residue that Sanders claimed to have was proven to be fraudulent. He illegally obtained the residue by having a pilot steal fabric of an airline seat from the investigation site. In addition, the FBI later concluded after testing the residue that it was only upholstery glue.

Nonetheless, the missile theory has maintained some staying power with a number of proponents. In April 1999, a retired military officer and aviation mishap analyst named William S. Donaldson wrote a letter to the Boeing

Company and TWA. He contended that from the beginning of the crash there had been a massive governmental cover-up, and that witnesses with irrefutable proof have been silenced or discredited.

Donaldson wrote that there are over "107 witnesses on 4 aircraft, 19 boats, and 31 locations ashore," who have all given eyewitness proof of seeing a missile on the night Flight 800 went down. In the letter, Donaldson focuses on a missile ejector motor can that a crewman on the fishing vessel *Alpha Omega* found. Every missile has an ejector can that looks like a soda can, and a find like the *Alpha Omega*'s would be proof that a missile went off that night. Unfortunately, the can was not examined, as the fisherman who found it did not know its significance and tossed it back into the sea. If it had been examined, it could have been determined if it was a military-issue ejector can based on small distinguishing marks that indicate the can's manufacturer.

It wasn't until November 1996 that FBI agents finally began questioning members of the fishing crew. A crewman identified a sample ejector can brought to him by the FBI as somewhat similar to what he'd found a month earlier. He recognized two distinctive wires attached to the can. After the interview with the fisherman, the NTSB started a trawling operation and contracted scallop boats that were to be manned by FBI agents. The purpose was to discover if any missile ejector motor cans could be found. The search operation was abruptly shut down in April 1997 and nothing more was revealed.

The terrorist bomb theory was also actively investigated. This theory seemed the most plausible in the beginning of the investigation, given the other acts of terrorism that were reported in the news. Although according to Britain's Center for the Study of Terrorism and Political Violence, state-sponsored terrorist incidents declined from 73 in 1988 to 10 in 1994, the recent June 1996 truck bombing of U.S. troops in Saudi Arabia made Americans suspect that terrorism had struck again. Also, initially there seemed to be so many similarities between TWA Flight 800 and Pan Am Flight 103, which experts proved was downed by a terrorist bomb attack in 1988.

The terrorist bomb theory was the least popular because the main cause for its support came from an unreliable source. Before the crash, the London office of an Egyptian newspaper, *Al Hayat*, had received a written warning that a group of Islamic militants was about to "deliver the ultimate response to the threats of the foolish American president." The threat added that people "will be amazed as to the size of that response."

This message was relayed to Washington, where the State Department ascertained that the group was called "The Movement for Islamic Change/The Jihad Wing of the Arabian Peninsula." This splinter group had already claimed to be responsible for the November 1995 bomb attack in Riyadh, Saudi Arabia, that claimed the lives of five Americans and two Indians.

Yet in spite of this message, a senior official with the FBI stated, "If we thought that this letter was linked in some way to the TWA crash we would not be fulminating against it." Though the FBI did not believe that this group's threat had anything to do with the crash of Flight 800, they were open to other possibilities and so they immediately turned the probe into an international criminal investigation. They planned to recover and analyze the voice and flight data recorders from the plane, which would be the most decisive in proving a terrorist attack.

Along with the voice and data recorders it was also necessary for the FBI to find some evidence of explosive residue from the wreckage of the aircraft. The remains

of TWA Flight 800 were at the bottom of the sea, but once the parts of the plane were brought to the surface, forensic experts claimed that finding such residue was possible and that it would serve as conclusive evidence.

But in 1997, ten months after the crash when 90 percent of the plane had been retrieved from the ocean floor, FBI director Louis Freeh appeared on NBC's *Meet the Press* in May. He finally stated, "The evidence is certainly not moving in the direction of a terrorist attack. It is, in fact, moving in the other direction. I think the evidence as we have developed it, and particularly the evidence we have not found, leads to the conclusion this was a catastrophic mechanical failure."

The difficulty in eliminating the bomb theory as the

Crash investigators inspect the nose section of Pan Am Flight 103, which was taken down by a bomb in 1988 over Scotland. Those who believed a bomb caused the Flight 800 explosion pointed out the similarities between the two disasters.

During the summer of the TWA 800 tragedy, Americans had enough reason to suspect the crash had resulted from a terrorist attack. Just a month before, a truck bomb had blasted a military housing complex in Dharan, Saudi Arabia, the remains of which are pictured here.

cause of the crash was that there were similarities in the voice and flight data recorders retrieved from Flight 800, and those of Pan Am's Flight 103 and Air India's Flight 182, which both had been downed by a bomb. All three of the data recorders indicated "evidence of a massive catastrophic failure consistent with an explosive device." But in spite of these similarities, the investigators still could not find any bomb residue in Flight 800.

The last theory was that the plane had a mechanical

problem. One of the first items that investigators look for in establishing mechanical failure is the set of large pins that bolt the turbine engines to the wings of the plane. Investigators cited the failure of these pins as the cause of the earlier crash of an El Al cargo jet in the Netherlands, so investigators conjectured this mechanical failure could have caused Flight 800's crash.

The first problem with this theory was that in the El Al crash, there had been no reports of the "massive fireball" that from the start eyewitnesses described with regard to Flight 800. Neither was there any evidence in the El Al crash of a sudden shutdown in the voice and data recorders, which would occur in the event of some major mechanical failure, such as loss of electricity. In addition, no one at the NTSB could remember an instance in which a plane had just exploded without warning from a mechanical malfunction. Some more tangible evidence was necessary if the FBI and the NTSB would blame the disaster on a mechanical failure.

Finding the Answers

6

Before anyone could come up with any definitive answers as to what had caused the Flight 800 crash, an extensive investigation had to begin, which required that the entire plane be brought up from the depths of the sea. The NTSB—which was accused of delaying the investigation—insisted that before anything could be retrieved it needed to make an extensive analysis of the untouched wreckage. The NTSB also argued that ascertaining exactly where the plane was when it went into the water would enable the group to determine statistics vital to piecing together the cause of the crash. The board first needed to make a careful video analysis of the wreckage field.

The navy immediately became involved in assisting the NTSB and the FBI in what was called "the largest salvage operation since the one following the attack on Pearl Harbor." By the end of the investigations, officials would put the cost of the salvage operation at well over $8 million. The navy would end up assisting in the recovery of the remains of Flight 800 for 104 days. The recovery operation involved four navy ships, three navy-contracted vessels, and 225 divers at different times during the operation. Whatever remains the navy was able to find were transported to a hanger in Calverton, a town on Long Island, for analysis by various agencies. There, it became known as the Calverton investigation.

For the recovery operation, the U.S. Navy had contracted Oceaneering International Incorporated just four hours after the crash. The company sent several marine accident investigators with underwater search equipment to the crash site. Oceaneering International used a pinger locator system, which is dragged behind a boat trolling the waters of a crash site and is able to locate the signal emitted by the data recorder. Along with the pinger system Oceaneering sent remotely operated vehicles (ROVs) to the crash site to provide video images of the wreckage. Using the video and the sonar-equipped instruments together, divers would know exactly where to look.

The NTSB insisted that it perform its analysis of the underwater site before anyone interfered with it or removed anything. During the analysis, the NTSB also searched for the plane's black boxes. There was much excitement early on when servicemen of the Air National Guard were able to locate the exact position of the tail section of the plane. In most jet planes the black boxes are typically located in the tail section. The new find directed the NTSB's search immediately to this area.

The scientific evidence that the NTSB and FBI needed was slow in being gathered, however. A full week

had passed before there was any sign of recovering the plane's black boxes. The pinger system initially thought to be so effective was proving unsuccessful. A new plan evolved that would use the technology of the navy ship named the USS *Grasp*. This ship utilized scanners and video cameras, which the divers hoped would be able to locate the black boxes.

It was only when one of the navy divers from the USS *Grasp* spotted a box with "Flight Recorder" stenciled on its side that the boxes were finally brought to the surface. Representatives from the NTSB on board the USS *Grasp* watched the retrieval of the boxes on a video camera. The ship was full of elated people.

The navy, leading the salvage operation after the Flight 800 crash, commissioned the USS *Grasp* as a diving platform for the retrieval of victims and wreckage.

Having recovered the cockpit voice recorder (CVR) and flight data recorder (FDR)—together called "the black boxes"—the painstaking task of analyzing every detail contained in them began. Everyone anticipated that the answer to what happened to Flight 800 would be known after the data from the boxes were analyzed. This task fell to Dennis Grossi and Jim Cash at NTSB headquarters, who review flight data recorders and then translate the information from them into a language that investigators can understand.

The high hope that these boxes would bring answers was quickly dispelled. Grossi and Cash analyzed the tapes with excruciating attention to detail. The tapes had recorded every action of the plane's activity from the moment of take-off, as well as any conversations within the flight deck. According to Cash, there was nothing revealing on the tape. "The most intriguing part was the lack of anything intriguing," he said. "Usually, something is going on before. The crew will say something or there's other indications going on. In this one, everything was perfectly normal, just the noise at the end and that's it." The "noise at the end" referred to a split-second sound at the end of the tape.

For three days the tapes were subjected to a variety of sophisticated tests in the hope of producing some conclusions about the "noise." But eventually, Cash had to inform the NTSB that he and Grossi could come to no conclusions about the tapes at all.

Once the black boxes had been located and brought to the surface, and the cameras on both the USS *Grasp* and the Oceaneering ship had taken detailed photographs of the wreckage site, the gruesome task of bringing up the victims' remains began. The plane's wreckage and the victims rested 104 feet below the surface of the ocean and nine miles off the coast of Long Island, encompassing a search site approximately a quarter of a mile wide. The USS *Grasp* was kept in operation to ferry divers down to the search area that was designated as "Box A." Andrew Gliganic, a diver from the Suffolk County, N.Y., Police Department, described how he and other divers dealt with the grim task of bringing up the remains of passengers. "Emotionally, we are disconnecting so that we can do our job," he said.

In the first days after the crash, the difficult task assigned to the divers was made even more complicated by the rough sea conditions off Long Island. The choppy waters and the high winds made retrieving either the passengers' remains or the wreckage itself very difficult. Deep Drone 7200, a robot with a camera and remote control capabilities, was brought into the search. With the help of the Deep Drone 7200, the team finally located a part of the cockpit. This find was of great importance to the crash investigators and James Kallstrom, the FBI's chief investigator, who afterwards said, "I just think that somewhere in the front of the plane is a clue." It was around this time that people believed that like Pan Am Flight 103, Flight 800's crash was caused by a terrorist bomb attack. Kallstrom commented on this possibility: "The FBI is not rooting for a bomb. The best thing for the country and probably for the world is a mechanical failure."

On July 19, 1996, Kallstrom announced that in an effort to gather any and all information about the crash, the FBI Joint Terrorism Task Force operating out of New York was requesting citizens of Long Island and anyone else with specific information about the disaster to call an 800 number or contact a website specifically set up for the investigation. The FBI had tried this approach before with major bombing investigations, and had been very impressed by a response received from a 14-year-old

When divers had difficulty tracking down all of the Flight 800 wreckage, the navy used the Deep Drone 7200, a state-of-the-art robot with a remote-controlled camera that helped find the plane's cockpit.

boy in Guatemala. In June 1996, he logged on to the FBI website and sent an E-mail informing the agency of a neighbor he thought might be on the site's Ten Most Wanted Fugitives list. He turned out to be correct. The FBI hoped that by putting its site out and asking for information regarding the TWA 800 disaster, someone might come forward with something that would help investigators find the answers they so desperately needed.

Actually, answers to what had downed the huge jet-liner were quickly coming in from all directions from the moment the plane went down. Bernard Loeb, the Director of Aviation Safety, heard about the crash of TWA Flight 800 and immediately, like many others, came to the conclusion that it was caused by a bomb.

After Loeb and his team arrived at the site and began the investigation, however, he began to reassess his opinion. "Crimes are corroborated fairly quickly," he said. "Organizations take credit, law enforcement hears something, the wreckage reveals something, the CVR gives clues. We weren't getting anything to suggest that a criminal enterprise had taken place. No evidence from the floating debris, no pitting or gas washing on the metal. The bodies gave us no evidence, no fragments or materials. There was no shred of evidence telling us this could be a crime." Loeb even started giving interviews to the media, and appeared on CBS's *60 Minutes,* saying that the crash of Flight 800 was "probably a mechanical issue."

Loeb was not completely correct in stating that there was "not a shred of evidence." FBI investigators had in the weeks after the crash discovered a minute amount of bomb residue in the plane wreckage. They thought an explosive had caused the crash until they were notified that Flight 800 had once been used in a training exercise for bomb-sniffing dogs.

On June 10, 1996, the St. Louis airport police reported, they had trained their dogs in the plane. The exercise involved placing ten packages of explosive chemicals inside the craft so that the bomb dogs could find them. The chemicals used in that test were the very same ones that were found in the minute traces of residue on the Flight 800 wreckage that had baffled investigators.

As investigators started ruling out other answers, Loeb increasingly became convinced that the crash was caused when the center fuel tank of the plane exploded. This theory was borne out when Loeb consulted Merritt Birky, a chemist who had done extensive investigations into the mechanics of how the plane's fuel tanks work.

A state trooper watches a bomb-detecting German shepherd sniff baggage in an airport lounge. Investigators thought they found evidence of bomb residue in the Flight 800 wreckage until they realized that the residue was used in an earlier training exercise for bomb-sniffing dogs.

Merritt Birky had been working for NTSB as an explosion investigator. He had just finished an investigation of a grain storage container that exploded when a spark of static ignited the mix of grain and air. The blast from that explosion was strong enough to rip away steel walls. When he heard that Flight 800 had left New York with its center fuel tank all but empty, it made the chemist wonder if there were enough vapors in the almost empty tank to turn it into a bomb.

Boeing, the manufacturer of the 747 that was Flight 800, did not believe it was possible for the plane to self-destruct in this manner. To prove the theory wrong, the company leased a 747-100 to recreate the scenario of Flight 800 as Birky and Loeb had suggested. Five weeks after the crash of Flight 800, Boeing outfitted a plane with temperature gauges inside the fuel tank, let it sit with the air packs running, and then flew it up to 13,700 feet. The test results showed that "the tank could get hot, hot enough to have an explosive brew in the tank before the plane ever left the ground." Birky commented on the test. "It explained the accident," he said. "You can have a flammable mix in the tank. If there's an ignition source, it will blow up. It will blow the plane out of the sky."

But it wasn't until the spring of 1997 that a possible ignition source could be identified, and it came from an unforeseen place. Tower Air, an all-747 carrier from New York, had called the FAA to report that a maintenance worker had seen indications of a short circuit in the center fuel tank on one of its planes. Upon examining the residue left on the wiring parts involved in that short circuit, the FAA noticed that this residue was the same as a mysterious, as yet unidentified residue that had been found on the wiring of Flight 800. Amazingly, it was not until three years later that the FAA finally subjected the material to testing, which revealed startling results. When scientists applied 170 volts to the wiring, it caused the residue to "flash and make a popping sound that could be heard across the lab." This was more than enough proof that the residue in Flight 800 could have been ignited and would have had enough force to then ignite the vapors in the center fuel tank of the plane.

What is incredible is that the FAA had a record of 13 similar fuel tank explosions on commercial aircrafts over the past 35 years, yet it had deemed the hazard an acceptable risk. FAA director of aircraft certification Tom McSweeny said that people have known for years that planes carry around fuel that can explode. "At the time we did not see a critical safety issue," he stated.

Meanwhile, the military certainly knew about the hazards of fuel tank explosions. In the air force, 747s are called E-4s, and are used by the military as communication and operations centers in national emergencies. In 1979, the air force, which had just started to use the E-4s, asked Boeing to investigate a problem involving the center tank of the plane getting very hot and causing the engines to shut down. In 1980, Boeing responded by making some changes, and the matter went no further. The investigations into the crash of TWA Flight 800 would change all that.

For the investigators to come to a definite conclusion that an ignition source caused the center tank to ignite and blow up the 747, they had to examine each and every part of the downed plane. To accomplish this task, the remains of TWA Flight 800 were taken to an abandoned aircraft manufacturing plant in Riverhead, Long Island, and separated in two hangers. The larger of the two hangers housed the remains of the plane's fuselage, and the second contained the remains of the cabin section of the plane. Once the plane had been brought there the investigations at the Calverton hanger began in earnest. With the NTSB and the FBI both examining the remains of the plane, it was an uncomfortable union from the start, as each had differing theories on what had caused the crash. At the beginning of the investigations, the NTSB maintained it would be able to prove from forensic evidence that mechanical failure of some kind caused the crash; the FBI still believed it could prove a bomb brought the plane down.

Speculations into the missile theory continued still, especially in September 1999 when the magazine *Insight on the News* published new radar data recorded on the night of the crash. The magazine received a floppy disk from an unidentified source at the NTSB. The radar data on this particular disk showed radar blips of activity near the area where Flight 800 went down. The public was informed about an earlier disk with original data that showed little activity, and which would support the government claim that there was no military exercise taking place in the area that night. The second disk held data that *Insight* had plotted with the help of an independent radar technician. According to the magazine, the disk showed "in excess of two dozen surface vessels and aircraft detected by radar just beyond the 20-nautical-mile mark." It also showed two aircraft just outside the boundary heading towards Area W-105, the military exercise zone in close proximity to the TWA 800 crash site. Information of this nature gave credence to both the friendly fire theory and accusations of a government cover-up.

For all the conclusions that the FBI and NTSB were making, it seemed that other investigators were finding completely different answers.

Unanswered Questions

T he crash of TWA Flight 800 was voted the biggest news story of
1996. According to the vote made by broadcast news directors and
newspaper editors in an Associated Press poll, the story eclipsed
the outcome of the presidential election, the arrest of the Unabomber, the
crash of ValuJet 592 in the Florida Everglades, and the bombing in Atlanta,
Georgia, during the Summer Olympics. It may even have been the story of
the decade, because well into 1997 and the following years the public would
devour any news of Flight 800.

In November 1997, James Kallstrom wrote a letter to the families of the
230 people who lost their lives on Flight 800. It stated: "Every possible lead
has been covered, all possible avenues of investigation exhaustively
explored and every resource of the U.S. government has been brought to

bear." The investigation reached the conclusion that "there was no evidence that Flight 800 was brought down intentionally." There was no reason to believe that a terrorist bomb or that any fire—friendly or otherwise—brought down TWA Flight 800.

This left only the mechanical failure theory as the cause for the crash of Flight 800. Investigators felt that their probe must delve into the center fuel tank, which had to be involved in a mechanical failure of such explosive force.

Methods to prevent fuel tank explosions had been available to the aviation industry for some time. The industry had known about fuel tanks being subject to explosions since 1963, when Pan Am's Flight 214 went down after an in-flight explosion. After the crash, Pan Am captain Eugene Banning, the Airline Pilots Association's air safety investigator, had been called out to investigate. Eyewitnesses to that crash had reported that they'd seen lightning and indeed the weather that night was stormy. But experts testified that they had never heard of lightning destroying a plane in flight.

The crash of Pan Am's Flight 214 became instant news primarily because it was the first time a Pan Am plane had crashed in the five years the company had been flying planes. Investigations into what had caused the plane to crash turned up disturbing information about the crash of a TWA Lockheed plane even earlier in 1959. In the TWA crash, lightning had also hit the plane, which experts determined ignited vapors in an empty fuel tank, causing the plane to explode. The only conclusion that could be drawn from these findings was that lightning was not a serious threat to planes in and of itself, but that there was an inherent danger of having vapor in the fuel tanks. The Civil Aeronautics Board (CAB) issued a statement in 1963 urging the prohibition of flammable jet fuels and "asking for the development of a method to prevent explosions by removing the oxygen from airplane fuel tanks." This process is known as inerting.

In November 1964, a TWA 707 plane, also flying as TWA Flight 800, was continuing its flight from Rome to Athens when the pilot aborted take-off. The plane should have been clear from danger, but its wing hit an obstruction near the runway, causing fuel to spill from the wing tank. The center section ignited and the plane erupted in flames. Passengers in the rear of the plane were able to escape through back exits, but those in the center of the plane where the fuel tanks exploded never had a chance. The CAB recommendations on inerting had never been followed.

In the wake of these tragic disasters, Pan Am stopped using the more flammable of the jet fuels for its planes and TWA soon followed. But for several years, no airline made any moves to use the inerting process that had been recommended along with the call for different jet fuel. In a 1968 speech to fellow pilots, Eugene Banning said, "The cost to provide this protection is not high, not cheap either, but certainly not as expensive as the TV, movies, music and other frills. . . . Would the public, if given a choice, choose movies or a good fuel explosion prevention system?"

In a sworn deposition given after the crash of Flight 800, the U.S. Air Force's Bill Brookley recounted a conversation he'd had with Boeing's Don Nordstrom, who in 1969 was in charge of the certification of the fuel systems on 747s. Nordstrom indicated that cost was always a major factor with the manufacturing company. Brookley claimed that Nordstrom told him, "They (Boeing) could afford to lose an airplane with a couple of hundred passengers every ten years, and it would still not cost as much . . . as it would to install a nitrogen inerting system on a fleet of aircraft and support it for ten years." Nordstrom, of course, denied ever making such a statement.

But the fact remained that even from as far back as 1977, Boeing had no intentions of pursuing the installation of inerting systems in their planes. In that year a crash involving two 747s took place in Tenerife in the Canary Islands. In a hearing following the incident, Boeing spokesperson Fred Grenich stated, "Our evidence was strong enough, and in my mind we presented over-whelming evidence that liquid nitrogen inerting was not viable for commercial use."

Even though this may have been true with the early inerting systems, the technology was advancing and studies into OBIGGS (Onboard Inert Gas Generating Systems) were making inerting more feasible. In 1981, the air force even starting to use OBIGGS on its planes and gave the contract to Boeing to implement those changes. Fred Grenich, ironically, was now one of the engineers assigned to the project for the military. Grenich and others tried to interest the FAA in their studies and the technological advances that had been made with developing inerting systems that were less cumbersome and more cost-effective.

Tragically, it wasn't until after the 1996 crash of TWA Flight 800 that anyone outside of the military would listen to how inerting systems could be installed into commercial planes without costing the manufacturers and operators too much. By 1996, Grenich had left his job working for the military and was reassigned to Boeing's commercial sector. He got a call from Ivor Thomas, a fellow colleague, who asked Grenich to join an in-house task force to find out what caused Flight 800 to explode. "Dust off your old data on fuel tank inerting," Thomas told him. "I think we're going to need it."

According to the results of that in-house investiga-tion, Boeing had failed to locate the cause of the mid-air

In August 2000, the NTSB held a meeting to discuss the findings from its extensive investigation. Chairman Jim Hall appears on the large screen above the officials.

explosion. The report went on to state that there was no evidence to suggest that the plane had been shot down by a missile, or that it had been the victim of a terrorist bomb attack. Boeing's report to the NTSB was given in April of 2000, and it stated that the crash was caused by "an ignition of flammable vapors in the center wing tank, resulting in a loss of structural integrity of the aircraft." Boeing declined to determine the source of that "ignition" and left it to the NTSB to solve.

In August 2000, NTSB official Bernard Loeb explained that the most probable cause of the crash involved the wiring system leading to the center fuel tank. A short circuit from higher-voltage wires could allow excessive voltage to be sent to the tank through the fuel quantity indication wires. Loeb added that nothing was absolutely certain, but of all the ignition scenarios investigated, this one was the most likely.

In the wake of these conclusions, Boeing asked the airline industry to make some changes. According to an August report in *Airline Industry Information*, the new information led to "new safety recommendations for fuel tank systems and the operation of air conditioning onboard while aircraft are parked at airports." Boeing admitted that running the air conditioners as long as TWA did might have created the fatal fuel vapors. The final verdict on the crash of Flight 800 was that it was caused by an explosion in the center fuel tank resulting from heated fuel vapors, with an ignition source in the plane's wiring. For the investigators, their work was done.

As the official investigation closed so did the poignant story on one of the smallest items found among the wreckage. Divers at the site had almost immediately found floating amongst the deluge of debris a small jewel box containing a diamond ring. Investigators figured that a small piece of bubble wrap in the box must have kept it afloat. Until a friend sent Julie Stuart a photo of a ring that had appeared in a French magazine article covering the crash, she had thought it was lost forever. Julie's fiancé, Andrew Krukar, was a passenger on Flight 800 and was planning to meet Julie in Paris where he would give her the ring. After seeing the photo and recognizing the ring as the one her fiancé was about to give her, she faxed to James Kallstrom 11 pages of documentation to prove she was the rightful owner.

It took almost a year, but finally on December 23, 1997, Julie Stuart met with James Kallstrom at his FBI office, where he presented her with the ring. It had remained in FBI custody as evidence ever since it had been found after the crash.

James Sanders, who had called the Flight 800 investigation a government conspiracy, was not treated so kindly. He and his wife Elizabeth were tried and convicted for conspiring to steal Flight 800 wreckage. Their sentence, coming three years after the crash of Flight 800, was probation.

Pierre Salinger, who claimed to have proof that Flight 800 had been shot down by friendly fire, recanted and admitted that he found out that the information on which

James Sanders and his wife Elizabeth, proponents of the missile theory, speak with reporters before a pretrial hearing in 1999. The couple was later convicted of conspiring to steal evidence from the Flight 800 wreckage.

he had based his claim had proven to be an Internet hoax.

Although the official investigations ended, the grieving families today still struggle through the long aftermath of the disaster. Some face legal entanglements with insurance companies, which many feel have not paid adequate compensation to the victims' families. Because TWA Flight 800 was an international flight, damage awards under the Warsaw Convention rules of 1929 are limited to "$75,000 per victim unless an airline can be shown to be guilty of willful misconduct." Additionally, when a plane crashes at sea, U.S. maritime law applies. In that case, only wives and dependent children can claim damages. "That's a double whammy," said San Francisco lawyer Gerald Sterns. "Not only do you have the $75,000 cap but you also have the law of the high seas. Where does that leave high-school students from Mountoursville, PA? Legally their lives have no value."

Larger settlements are possible if the airline is found to be at fault either as a result of mechanical failure or improperly instituted security measures. For either of these to occur the investigators have to come up with some forensic evidence of mechanical failure or bomb residue. In the Pan Am Flight 103 crash, when investigators determined that a bomb had caused the crash, the 225 families settled with the airline for a reported $500 million.

Lee Kreindler of the law firm Kreindler & Kreindler was the chief plaintiff's lawyer in the Pan Am Flight 103 crash case. He also represented 25 of the families in the crash of TWA Flight 800 in their suit filed against Boeing and TWA. In the case against Pan Am, Boeing was not a party to the suit since that crash was attributed to a bomb.

In the ongoing case of TWA Flight 800 on March 30, 2000, the U.S. Second Circuit Court of Appeals handed down a ruling that allowed the families of the victims of the crash to seek higher damages against TWA and

Lee Kreindler, an accomplished plaintiff lawyer, agreed to represent 25 families of the victims of TWA Flight 800 in their case against TWA and Boeing, the plane's manufacturer.

Boeing. The ruling also affirmed that the crash occurred in U.S.-controlled waters and not on the "high seas," where international law protects airlines from heavy legal suits. This second ruling permitted families to make claims for punitive and emotional damages along with any monetary losses.

In August 2000, the Boeing Company made a public statement in its defense, saying that the NTSB recommendations had been followed and that the accident had been caused by potential maintenance problems, not by the manufacturing of the plane itself.

How Safe Are the Skies?

TWA was originally brought into service as Trans States Airlines in 1924. It was taken over by billionaire Howard Hughes, who was a major force in the airline industry. He renamed it Trans World Airways and under his leadership TWA became one of the first airlines to make scheduled flights to Europe.

In the 1980s, TWA was taken over by Carl Icahn and five years later it was forced into bankruptcy. The airline managed to avoid going out of business by bringing in outside investors, but after five more years it had to claim a second bankruptcy. After erasing $500 million in debts, TWA got out of bankruptcy once again and made a comeback.

By 1996, TWA was the seventh largest airline and boasted an almost 400% increase in earnings. It had just announced that it was about to lease

15 planes from McDonnell Douglas and was obtaining 10 new Boeing 757-200s. In 1996, TWA's problems did not seem to lie with its fleet of planes but with its finances.

But the traveling public is understandably more concerned with air safety than with an airline's financial status. TWA had been in operation some 72 years, and as an older airline operator it had a reputation for flying an older fleet of aircraft. In spite of their age, TWA's planes were considered safe and before the crash of Flight 800, TWA had what the industry considered an excellent safety record among U.S. airlines.

This did not mean that there had never been any fatalities abroad a TWA flight. On December 1, 1974, a TWA 727 flying into Washington's Dulles International Airport crashed into the Blue Ridge Mountains, killing all 92 passengers.

In another disaster in 1985, a terrorist bomb went off during a TWA flight from Rome to Greece and three passengers were sucked out of the plane. The remaining passengers managed to survive. In the same year, TWA found itself in the world spotlight when Middle Eastern hijackers held hostage the pilot of a TWA plane. In the ensuing deliberations, the terrorists shot and killed a passenger, U.S. Navy diver Robert Stethem, and threw his body from the plane while hundreds of news television cameras recorded the images for people to watch all over the world.

TWA was again in the media spotlight in 1993 when a TWA 727 crashed into a small private plane taking off in St. Louis. All passengers on the TWA flight were unharmed, but the two passengers of the small plane were killed.

The crash of TWA Flight 800 was often compared to the Lockerbie, Scotland, crash of Pan Am Flight 103 in 1988 because the two planes were the same model.

TWA was in severe financial straits in the 1980s until entrepreneur Carl Icahn took over the company and helped bring it out of bankruptcy.

After the deaths of 270 people on that flight, in addition to 14 on the ground, the public's fear of terrorism in the air reached an apex.

Two years after the Pan Am Flight 103 crash, Congress finally passed the Aviation Security Improvement Act, which tried to address the obvious need for increased security at airports. In the wake of the Lockerbie crash, it became evident that the measures airport security had

Before the Flight 800 crash, TWA had a troubled history, marked by the 1985 hijacking of a TWA plane in Lebanon. One passenger lost his life during the 17-day standoff.

in place were inadequate. Better methods and more sophisticated technology were necessary to detect bombs and other hazardous materials at airport security checkpoints.

This legislation required the FAA to develop technology necessary to detect explosive materials, and so in 1994 it certified the CTX-5000, made by InVision. The CTX-5000 is able to detect various explosive materials, which makes it more effective than earlier machines. However, it is also slower. The CTX-5000 can scan only 400 bags per hour, while older x-ray machines can scan 1,500 bags per hour. InVision senior vice president David Pillor explained the current dilemma: "Today's standards are meant to stop hijacking. They don't find bombs."

In spite of the shortcomings of the CTX-5000, three of them were being used in the United States in 1996, and Kennedy Airport had just ordered a fourth that had not yet been put into operation at the time of Flight 800's crash. The problem facing the airline industry was companies had to manage new security expenses and still remain competitive, keeping airfares low and affordable for the traveling public.

But explosive devices were not the only airline safety concern. Immediately following the crash of Flight 800, President Clinton had Vice President Al Gore head up a commission on airline safety. This commission, as Ed Block had done several years ago, asked the FAA to look into the electrical mechanics of current airliners. It could not have escaped Director of Aircraft Certification Tom McSweeny that this request was very similar to the one Block made in his letter to the FAA six years before.

It took yet another year before the FAA issued a report admitting that its investigations had proven that wire inspections were "too general." The report explained that there was "no systematic process to identify and address potential catastrophic failures caused by electrical faults of wiring systems aside from accident investigation associated activities."

This was a small comfort to the traveling public, which was basically hearing the FAA admit that it could not prevent disasters from occurring; it could only investigate the causes of disasters after they occurred. In view of this fact, the FAA formed the Aging Systems Task Force. After two years of analyzing the wreckage of Flight 800, the NTSB recommended the mandatory inspection and rewiring of the fuel tanks in the older Boeing 747 jets. NTSB chairman Jim Hall said that the board had found damaged wiring in the fuel gauge systems in a few of the older 747s in addition to TWA

Flight 800. In an interview in 1998, Hall would not state that the explosion of TWA Flight 800 was caused by faulty wiring, but he did concede that "unsafe conditions . . . may exist in other older B-747s and should be addressed by the Federal Aviation Administration."

Ed Block, who had been writing to the FAA since 1974 about potential problems with wiring, was given a seat on the Aging Systems Task Force Committee at the insistence of a newly formed consumer group called the National Air Disaster Alliance Foundation. The NADAF had formed in 1995 in Pittsburgh, Pennsylvania, and was comprised of family members and survivors of ten air crash groups. The mission statement of the NADAF is "to raise the standards of safety, security and survivability for commercial aviation passengers and to support victims' families." The NADAF was formed to specifically address the "grievances of all who have been affected by devastating air tragedies."

As a self-proclaimed "grassroots advocacy group," the NADAF quickly became the largest voice working for aviation safety. Relying only on donations to accomplish its goals, the group has grown in number since it began work in 1995. Incredibly, the NADAF has managed to accomplish great things and in 1996, its efforts led to the passing of the Aviation Disaster Family Assistance Act. This act established for the relatives of victims a "Family Advocate," a position that had not previously existed. The group also spearheaded the passage of another act called the Airplane Pilot Hiring Act, which requires airlines to perform a background check before hiring a pilot, and requires the FAA to establish minimum standards for pilot qualifications.

To accomplish its goal of improved airline safety, the NADAF studies the causes of previous fatal airline crashes and ascertains what safety measures are lacking.

It strives to make certain through the FAA that the airline industry implements these measures. It is hoped, of course, that these efforts will prevent future crashes and devastation for others.

Mary Schiavo, a former inspector general of the Department of Transportation and a well-known air safety advocate, spoke at one of the NADAF annual meetings. She stated that the NADAF "is the undisputed leader when it comes to objective, persistent, and heartfelt efforts. No one can question your place at the table. Your members have amassed a pool of knowledge that the government does not have and cannot replicate."

Schiavo joined many others in accusing the FAA of being lax for years. She expressed her distrust in the FAA's ability to monitor the safety of the traveling public. In her scathing editorial for *Newsweek* entitled "I Don't Like to Fly," she stated that she personally had to insist that a plane on which she was flying be taken out of service after she saw that mechanics were patching it up with tape. She also voiced her serious doubts about airline inspections, parts, and training, as well as the air traffic control system.

Part of her concern resulted from having just completed a security assessment of U.S. airports. Schiavo stated afterward she had reason to be "highly critical" of security, because her staff was able to penetrate airport security about 40 percent of the time. "My staff was able to, literally, get out on the tarmac, get on to planes, get in cockpits and witness a number of test devices go through security," she said. "And we are troubled by that. We found that a lot of it was just plain lax attitude."

The general public is constantly being assured that it is safer in the sky than in a car on the highway. In the wake of the crash of Flight 800, a *U.S. News & World Report* article confirmed that in spite of the tragedy,

"The U.S. represents half the world's airline travel and that its rate of serious accidents or mishaps is the lowest in the world, half that of Western Europe." Regardless of statistics like this one, however, many feel that they are not safe. Mary Schiavo, the NADAF, and others believe that a more active hands-on approach to dealing with the safety of our skies is the answer. It cannot be left to the government or the airlines, because they all have a personal agenda.

In an unprecedented move, Mary Schiavo made a special donation to the NADAF accompanied by the following statement: "I am making a donation to the NADAF of aviation corporate stocks that will be held in NADAF's trust account, which will enable your members as shareholders to attend those corporate meetings and publicly ask the tough questions. By law the Board of Directors is required to answer share-holder questions. If they do not know the answer they are required to find out and provide answers to you. You can be a force for change directly to the corporate officers who are responsible for the answers."

By making a donation like this one, Schiavo helped enable the members of the NADAF to be a legitimate presence at aviation industry board meetings and thus be more active in making sure that safety measures become fact and not just talk. In the same bulletin sent out by the NADAF announcing Schiavo's donation, organization president Gail Dunham wrote, "Each of us knows that what happened to us, should NEVER happen to anyone! As time goes on, we all painfully learn that most air crashes are very preventable disasters."

On July 17, 2000, some of the families of the victims of TWA Flight 800 took part in the groundbreaking of a donated site on Long Island. It has become the site of a $1.5 million memorial for the 230 people who lost their lives in

the 1996 crash. Boeing promised to donate $100,000 to the construction of the memorial. To help raise the $600,000 still needed for the memorial's completion, engraved bricks for the pathway were for sale. The families envisioned the completed memorial as a 12-foot curved piece of granite engraved with the victims' names on one side and 230 doves facing the sea on the other. The stone would stand at Smith Point Park in Shirley, New York, the site of an existing memorial park, which is at the beach point closest to the crash site.

On July 17, 2000, four years after the crash, families and friends of the Flight 800 victims laid out roses and 230 candles at a memorial park in Shirley, New York.

TWA has not contributed to the building of the memorial. TWA spokesman Mark Abels explained that the airline and its insurance carrier had spent $13 million on funerals, memorial services, and travel arrangements for the grieving families. In his letter to John Seaman, who lost a niece in the crash and is head of "The Families of TWA Flight 800 Association," Abels wrote: "As time has gone on, we have found it increasingly difficult to support group activities, simply because the interests of the families differ and what comforts some invariably distresses others."

Years after the crash and after all the investigations have been put aside, there still remains a shroud of mystery and suspicion around the crash of TWA Flight 800. Some still claim there was a massive governmental cover-up and conspiracy at work. On July 17, 2000, a group of independent investigators who support the missile theory filed a suit in a district court in Spring-field, Massachusetts. They claimed several government agencies had refused to reveal their findings about the accident. According to a report from *Airline Industry Information*, "The Flight 800 Independent Researchers Organization has alleged that government authorities have refused requests for radar data and the analysis of metal found in crash victims' bodies and therefore violated the Freedom of Information Act." This group also claimed that the government had hidden or altered information in order to conclude that a center fuel tank explosion caused the crash.

Perhaps we will never really know what happened with TWA Flight 800. But it is probable that there was a conspiracy of silence with regards to not implementing known safety measures in planes. In his book *The Final Call*, British aviation journalist Steven Barlay said, "There are no new types of air crashes—only people with short memories. Every accident happens either because some-body did not know where to draw the vital dividing line between the unforeseen and the unforeseeable or because well-meaning people deemed the risk acceptable."

The efforts and continued work of those in the NADAF and other similar consumer advocacy groups provide the aviation industry with a group of people who have a long memory. They also present themselves as an identifiable force to be reckoned with. They ask the questions, get the answers, and break through the wall of silence that had shrouded the aviation industry. In so doing, they make the skies safer for us all.

Chronology

1985 Air India Flight 182 explodes over the Atlantic Ocean, killing 329 passengers

1988 A terrorist bomb destroys Pan AM Flight 103 over Lockerbie, Scotland, killing 270 passengers

1990 Aviation Security Improvement Act is passed, requiring the Federal Aviation Administration (FAA) to develop better technology to spot bombs in baggage

1994 FAA certifies the CTX-5000, a machine developed by InVision Technologies to detect gel, liquid, metal, plastic, and other kinds of explosive devices

1996 *July 17*: The London office of the Egyptian newspaper *Al Hayat* receives a fax warning of terrorist acts from Islamic militants just hours before Flight 800 is due to depart for Paris; the flight departs John F. Kennedy airport in New York at 8:19 P.M. and disappears from radar 12 minutes later

July 18: FBI agents and members of the New York Police Department anti-terrorism task force begin to interview hundreds of crash eyewitnesses from East Moriches, New York; James Kallstrom (FBI assistant director in charge), Charles Welti (Suffolk County medical examiner), and Robert Francis (vice chairman of the National Transportation Safety Board) jointly announce at a press meeting that it will take some time before they can make a definitive analysis of the crash

July 19: President Clinton meets with reporters and states that the government is doing its best to recover bodies and determine the cause of the accident; FBI creates a temporary website and asks the general public to e-mail tips or information about the crash of Flight 800

July 24: Marine investigators begin searching the ocean floor to find clues about the Flight 800 crash

August 5: U.S. navy commissions the salvage ship the USS *Grasp,* which will bring divers to the crash site to retrieve victims and evidence

September: Journalist Tonice Sgrignoli is charged with criminal impersonation after posing as a relative of someone in the crash of Flight 800; NTSB and FBI publicly deny allegations that there are any cover-ups dealing with the investigation

October 21: Lawyers for 25 families of victims file suit against Boeing and TWA, alleging that a preventable mechanical failure caused the crash

November 18: The government denies that a navy missile accidentally shot down Flight 800; the FBI discounts the "friendly fire" theory

December 23: The NTSB investigation finds that TWA Flight 800 crashed accidentally and that an explosion did occur in the center fuel tank, possibly caused by an electrical spark; the finding persuades the victims' families to file massive lawsuits

1997 *January 4*: The TWA Flight 800 disaster is voted the biggest news story of the year in an Associated Press poll

January 11: NTSB proposes a series of safety measures that it wants the FAA to implement by March 1997

December 23: James Kallstrom gives Julie Stuart, fiancée of crash victim Andrew Krukar, the engagement ring Krukar intended for her in a private ceremony at the New York FBI office

Bibliography

Books and Periodicals

Acohido, Byron. "Suit Against Boeing, TWA in Works." *The Seattle Times*, October 11, 1996.

Fedarko, Kevin. "A Theory Gone to the Dogs." *Time*, September 30, 1996.

Donaldson, William S. Letter to the Boeing Company. April 5, 1999. Available at http://www.allnatural.com/twa800.html.

Duffy, Brian, and Katherine T. Beddingfield. "The Sound of Silence." *U.S. News & World Report*, August 15, 1996.

"EmergencyNet News 'Flash' Report." July 17, 1996.

Liu, Melinda, and John Barry. "Watching and Waiting." *Newsweek*, August 26, 1996.

Milton, Pat. *In the Blink of an Eye: The FBI Investigation of TWA Flight 800*. New York: Random House, 1999.

Negroni, Christine. *Deadly Departure.* New York: Harper Collins, 2000.

"NTSB Rules Out Criminal Act as Cause of TWA Flight 800 Crash." *Airline Industry Information*, August 23, 2000.

O'Meara, Kelly Patricia. "New Radar Data, New Questions." *Insight on the News*, September 20, 1999.

"Overseas Pioneer TWA Has Good Safety Record." *USA Today*, November 13, 1996.

"Remarks on the Aircraft Tragedy in East Moriches, New York." *Weekly Compilation of Presidential Documents*, July 22, 1996.

Rist, Curtis. "Destiny's Gift." *People Weekly*, January 13, 1997.

Rosenblatt, Roger. "Death on a Summer's Night." *Time*, July 29, 1996.

———. "Personal Effects: Quogue Postcard." *The New Republic*, August 12, 1996.

Smith, Kyle. "A Separate Peace." *People Weekly*, July 28, 1997.

Wolper, Allan. "Persistent Pierre." *Editor & Publisher*, April 19, 1997.

Further Reading

Barlay, Stephen. *Cleared for Take-Off: Behind the Scenes of Air Travel.* North Pomfret, Vermont: Trafalgar Square, 1996.

Cohen, Susan, and Daniel Cohen. *Pan Am 103: The Bombing, the Betrayals, and a Bereaved Family's Search for Justice.* New York: NAL, 2000.

Milton, Pat. *In the Blink of an Eye: The FBI Investigation of TWA Flight 800.* New York: Random House, 1999.

Negroni, Christine. *Deadly Departure.* New York: Harper Collins, 2000.

Sanders, James. *The Downing of Flight 800.* New York: Kensington Publishing, 1997.

Websites

CNN. "Profile of TWA N93119."
http://www.cnn.com/US/9707/twa.800/what.wrong/profile.html

TWA Flight 800 Disaster: Cover-up?
http://www.all-natural.com/twa800.html

Families of TWA Flight 800 Assoc., Inc.
http://www.members.aol.com/hseaman275/newslttr.html

Federal Bureau of Investigation
http://www.fbi.gov

National Transportation Safety Board
http://www.ntsb.gov

Index

Index

Picture Credits

page

2: Mark Lennihan/AP/Wide World Photos

10: Bebeto Matthews/AP/Wide World Photos

14: Venanzio Raggi/AP/Wide World Photos

17: Mark Lennihan/AP/Wide World Photos

18-19: U.S. Navy/AP/Wide World Photos

23: Shawn Dowd, Rochester Democrat & Chronicle Photo/ AP/Wide World Photos

25: AP/Wide World Photos

28: Alex Wong/Newsmakers

30: Ron Frehm/AP/Wide World Photos

33: Reuters/Peter Morgan/ Archive Photos

35: Gail Burton/AP/Wide World Photos

37: Susan Ragan/AP/Wide World Photos

40: Leslie E. Kossoff/AP/Wide World Photos

45: Francois Mori/AP/Wide World Photos

49: InVision/AP/Wide World Photos

50: Michael Schmelling/ AP/Wide World Photos

52: Michel Lipchitz/AP/Wide World Photos

55: Ron Edmonds/AP/Wide World Photos

61: Dave Caulkin/AP/Wide World Photos

62: U.S. Navy/AP/Wide World Photos

64: Mark Wilson/AP/Wide World Photos

67: Charles L. Withrow, U.S. Navy/AP/Wide World Photos

70: Charles L. Withrow, U.S. Navy/AP/Wide World Photos

72: Susan Walsh/AP/Wide World Photos

76: Joe Marquette/AP/Wide World Photos

81: Kamenko Pajic/AP/Wide World Photos

83: Ed Betz/AP/Wide World Photos

85: Kathy Willens/AP/Wide World Photos

86: Joe Marquette/AP/Wide World Photos

89: Reuters/Jeff Christensen/ Archive Photos

90: Herve Merliac/AP/Wide World Photos

95: Ed Betz/AP/Wide World Photos

Front cover photo: AP Photo/Pool, John H. Cornell/© Reuters NewMedia Inc./Corbis
Back cover photo: AP Photo/Kathy Willens

BELINDA FRIEDRICH is a graduate of Randolph-Macon Women's College and is presently working on a master's degree in counseling. She worked for the *Caribbean Herald* as a columnist writing a weekly column entitled "Life in Paradise," and wrote a tourism book called *The Simple Guide to St. Maarten/St. Martin*. Belinda lives in South Carolina with her husband, Karl, and sons Karl-Desmond and Nickolas. This is her second book for Chelsea House.

JILL McCAFFREY has served for four years as national chairman of the Armed Forces Emergency Services of the American Red Cross. Ms. McCaffrey also serves on the board of directors for Knollwood—the Army Distaff Hall. The former Jill Ann Faulkner, a Massachusetts native, is the wife of Barry R. McCaffrey, formerly a member of President Bill Clinton's cabinet and director of the White House Office of National Drug Control Policy. The McCaffreys are the parents of three grown children: Sean, a major in the U.S. Army; Tara, an intensive care nurse and captain in the National Guard; and Amy, a seventh grade teacher. The McCaffreys also have two grandchildren, Michael and Jack.